Be a Parent

BONDING AND BUILDING FOR A LIFETIME

Christine Kiel Endicott

a common mom

Be a Parent

BONDING AND BUILDING

FOR A LIFETIME

By Christine Kiel Endicott

a common mom

Dedication

To every parent who questions their ability, seeks answers to be better, and wants proven examples of how to raise kind, confident, productive adults.

Acknowledgements

Much gratitude to my husband, Jay, who chose me 30 years ago and supports all my endeavors and without whom the children, and therefore this book, would not be possible. My editor, conspirator, friend and true love; thank you!

A special thanks to Heather Tyner Dongell who:

- Gave my kids a great start to their college experience.
- Listened to my stories of parenting young adults.
- Requested stories of parenting young children.
- Encouraged me to write this book.
- And whose editing and honest feedback helped produce the product you are now about to read.

To our parents: Jolene Endicott, Judy and Jim Kiel and Jim and Sunny Endicott who provided a great childhood and who continue to encourage our endeavors and help us through life's challenges.

Noel, Quinn and Rachel: May you find the wisdom you seek but more importantly, see the power you already possess in being able to raise your children well. Thank you for choosing the right paths and knowing when to get off the wrong ones. You all are my magnum opus and I am honored to be called your mom.

Table of Contents

Introduction

You most likely picked up this book because you want to be intentional about raising your kids but are unsure how to go about the task. In the next several pages I will unpack true stories of how my husband and I raised our children. I chose the chapters based on their developmental stages and in all honesty, the way their child-rearing days are separated in my memory. In each chapter I share a variety of ways we bonded with our children as they grew. You may choose to replicate these or develop your own ideas for how to better connect with each phase they are going through. I also highlight how we built them up from infancy to high school graduation; teaching them to use their manners, helping with household chores and choosing good friends and significant others. This is not an end-all-be-all answer to every parental question. It is a compilation of our lives raising three children, who came into the world less than 34 months apart and how we survived.

Whether you choose to continue to read this narrative of my personal thoughts and stories on parenting tips that worked for us, or whether you choose a different parental book, please get extra copies and share them with your parents or caregivers. It is a tremendous help if they can understand why you are choosing to parent the way you are, especially if it contradicts the way they were raised. Sharing your reasoning, discoveries, and wishes with your parents is important. You might be surprised how receptive they are. I have yet to meet a parent without regrets. We all have moments we wish we could take back, or things we think we should have done differently. If you were blessed to be raised by people who encouraged you, loved you for the unique person you are, and taught you the value of caring for others as well as the environment you live in, then you have a great advantage. Our home environment and random circumstances of life certainly shape who we become, and it can be difficult to break patterns of behavior (both good and bad) that habitually create our daily lives, but it is not impossible. I suppose that fact, in the end, is what pushed me to finally move forward with writing this book, that and my own reality of becoming a grandparent.

I wish to thank my children who, by the grace of God, felt my husband and I did a fine job raising them. They also asked me to write this book because they want to mimic that environment for their own children. It is difficult to write that sentence because I feel so inadequate. I know it was through daily prayer, my own positive upbringing, open communication and the partnership with my husband, Jay, that helped us succeed. It is also because of the constant help and encouragement of many friends and extended family that my children were able to enjoy a good childhood. Furthermore, I wish to thank Shane Warta, my office buddy for two years, who listened to my contemplations regarding my kids' teenage challenges as they transitioned between high school and adulthood. Shane encouraged me to write a book about my parenting ideas. And finally, I thank the random stranger who had a breakdown in the middle of the grocery aisle. I shared some encouraging words to help ease the challenge of her young children. I was puzzled by her abundant glee of my simple advice and enthusiastic comment: "You should write a book!" What seemed common sense to me was evidently not common to all.

I hope reading through this book will help you formulate an outline of a plan. That is all you need. The script will write itself, but if you have an outline of major issues and how you plan to discuss them within your family, the journey will be easier for all of you. If you know you want to raise a kind, confident, considerate adult, ask yourself, "What do I need to do to make them kind?" and "How can I create confidence?" Making a child happy is not our primary job. Happiness can be very fleeting. As a parent, our job is to teach them how to live a successful life in an unpredictable and changing world. Confidence will bring them peace. Proper boundaries to learn who they are will bring confidence. Providing encouragement and love will bring comfort, and helping them make wise choices that positively impact others will bring contentment and joy.

Having children is not about finding your purpose as a parent. It is not what you want *from* the children, but what you want to *give to them*. If you gain but one bit of wisdom that helps ease any phase of parenting, I will consider this a success. I am a common mom. And these pages are my stories and opinions of how my husband and I worked every day to bond with our children, build on their skills and raise kids who have become kind, productive and responsible adults.

Chapter 1: Infant
Be Intentional

"When you are intentional you choose to make decisions and take action on what's important to you. Being intentional means being clear upfront about what you want to achieve. You intentionally set out to achieve a specific outcome or result in the future that is important to you." (from lucemiconsulting. co.uk Being Intentional: 6 Ways to Be Intentional Every Day)

Congratulations! You have already made the first step towards being an intentional parent by reading this book. You are choosing to take action toward creating the outcome you want for the future: Raising a good kid. Being intentional means you are thinking about how to handle things. You discuss discipline with your spouse. You formulate a plan together that you can work on as a team throughout the life of your child. My mind naturally works in a strategic way, so this came easily for me. My husband works better "in the moment", so we had a good balance. A friend used to tease me about planning my kids' lives so far ahead I would miss what was currently happening. I responded that I would not be surprised by things because all the scenarios were already going through my mind. This is not true. Having my 3yr old go through a phase of going #2 in the yard one summer is not something I could foresee. Viewing my son at the top of a street light pole was quite unexpected. And when my 16 year old declared that she wanted to finish high school a semester early, I had to consciously hold my teeth together to prevent my jaw from dropping. Life is full of surprises, and life with children is a guaranteed creation of conundrums.

This is why it is so vital for you to have an intentional plan of how you want to parent. As you hold your infant and imagine the future for them, ask yourself questions about what skills and abilities they need to succeed. Innate qualities cannot be changed: Saying you want them to be fast, smart, and organized may not be qualities your child has when they are born. But you can help build habits into their lives which aid in growing wisdom, being tidy, or being athletic. More importantly, you can teach them how to be kind, productive, and confident by setting that example for them. Whether you choose to mimic my examples or use them as ideas to launch your own strategies for success is entirely up to you. Intentionally create your bonding moments and use them to build the bright future you are now imagining for your child.

Bonding

Give your baby massages. I read about this in *What to Expect the First Year* by Maria Masters and I chose to do this with my kids. We found it to be a very calming effect both for them, and for me. As you are changing their clothes, or when they are waking up from a nap, start with their head and gently rub around it. Speak to them, gently rub the eyebrows, cheek bones, jaws, ears and chin. Rub their tiny shoulders, arms and all the way out to each little finger. Rub their sides and tummy, the hips and legs, especially the joints and on to each toe. I discovered that my son was ticklish as he would squirm when I touched his ribs and my youngest daughter, who was always on the go, would lay very still and soak it all in. It only took a few minutes, but forced me to slow down as the tasks of each day can keep a young parent very busy. Once they reached mobility, this was no longer feasible as laying still for anything was not well tolerated. Physical touch is important in developing the brain of young children. Taylor Mallory Holland wrote "Hugging and other forms of nonsexual touching cause your brain to release oxytocin, known as the 'bonding hormone'. This stimulates the release of other feel-good hormones, such as dopamine and serotonin, while reducing stress hormones, such as cortisol and norepinephrine." (https://www.dignityhealth.org) You, being the one who provides healthy physical touch, will create a bond with them.

Read out loud. This should ideally start when you are pregnant, and both parents should participate. You do not need to read a children's book. It can be the newspaper, magazine article, or a post on social media. But read it out loud! They need to hear your voice. And yes, studies have shown that babies will respond to the sound of their parents' voices even hours out of the womb.

> Since the maternal voice is audible in utero, an infant starts to recognize their mother's voice from the third trimester The voice that they hear is muffled and low, and they can also hear their mother's heartbeat. Soon after birth, studies have shown that a baby will rec-

ognize their mother's voice and will expend great efforts to hear her voice better over unfamiliar female voices. This suggests that prenatal experiences influence a baby's ability to recognize their mother's voice. With continued exposure, your infant will become more familiar to the sound of other voices. They will start to recognize and form a preference to their father's voice, as well as other family and friends. *Does My Baby Recognize Me* - https://babyschool.yale.edu

I saw proof of voice recognition with my husband on the day our oldest was born. She was being a bit fussy, and I was exhausted so Dad took her out to the hallway hoping a walk would calm her. He softly began singing to her as he often did before she was born and she immediately stopped crying. She opened her eyes and stared at him as if saying, "Oh, this is familiar." The nurses all told me about it a few hours later and how sweet and touching it was to see her immediate reaction. I had a hymn I would sing to each child and then a short bedtime song that was unique to each of them. "Their song" will bring them to tears to this day if I sing it to them. Not a planned process. Just something that happened in the midst of creating routines, trying to make them feel special and helping them calm down to go to sleep.

Sing to them. You do not need to have an American Idol golden ticket to find success in this endeavor. Just hearing your voice brings a connection. You will find your own unique ways of bonding through music but only if you are brave enough to open your mouth and sing.

Music speaks to the soul in any language. My kids have many songs on their playlist that I crooned to when they were young because it brings back memories, feelings of home, and special times together. It creates a bond. I'll venture to guess that most of you, when you hear a familiar song, have at least one memory to go along with it. Music is a good thing. It beats the drowning noise of a television or the blaring silence of isolation. Turn on the music, and share a variety of it. I never listened to classical music until I had children, but it was popular in the late 90's and I actually found I enjoyed it. Expand your palate to something different on occasion and allow your child's brain to expand. Bond together by singing and dancing. My brother-in-law used to have a dance party with his kids each night to wear them out before bed. Our family is always making up silly words to familiar tunes. Share the music that moves you with your children. Most will cherish it the rest of their lives.

Building

Respond to them by teaching that their voice matters. Do not get me wrong. I am not advocating that you should run into the room every time your infant begins to fuss, but I am saying there is a fine balance between ignoring their pleas for help and displeasure vs. coddling them or training them to process that any noise gets a swift reaction. More than anything, this is the beginning of you understanding your child and communicating with them for the rest of their life.

You must study your child. Learn to identify their cry. And yes, to those newbies out there, you will have many different cries to decipher. A demanding cry "Hey, I am hungry!" An angry cry "I'm hot, or have a messy diaper." A scared or painful cry and a fussy cry. When your child is hungry or messy, of course you need to respond and take care of these needs. When your child is scared, comfort them. But know that there are times, like adults, that they may not know exactly what they want, or we may not be able to decipher that exact need. It is okay. It is completely okay to let them cry if you are feeling the breaking point and have done all you can. Perhaps your baby just needs space to cry it out without a panicked parent.

It took me nearly four months to realize that my son, when extremely tired, preferred to be left alone. He was the fussiest of my three children, and on one occasion in the midst of a screaming tirade, I needed to go to the bathroom. I laid him on the bed (as he was not rolling yet), and by the time I returned, he was peacefully asleep. I had never heard of putting a child in the crib while they were crying, but this is what he needed. The lady at the church nursery did not believe me when I told her, "If he gets really fussy, just put him in his car seat and lay a blanket over it. He prefers to be left alone when he is tired." She said when he got fussy she started to rock him and sing to him, but his cry escalated. She decided to try my advice and he quieted right down. Parents, study your child and you will become a successful parent. Recognizing and responding to their needs builds understanding.

Begin teaching: alphabet, language and colors. Some of you may have just rolled your eyes to the idea that you could begin teaching an infant such things. And I am not a trained expert on this. But I can tell you that I did these things for my children. They all began speaking and reading at a young age, and they all transitioned easily into school. Was that because I did the things which I am about to share, or was that because they had good genes? I can't answer that question, but I can tell you they plan to do the same thing with their children because they hope their kids can find equal success.

Place a "letter of the day" on the seat of the car as they face backwards. While you drive around, repeat that letter, the sounds it makes, find things that start with that letter as you drive along. Please do not let this take the place of conversations when others are riding with you. This is just a fun, simple thing I did to entertain myself as much as them. Believe me, I did not do it every day. In fact, I think M may have been the farthest down the alphabet I got with any of the kids. Some days I just needed music, or had no energy to bother with writing out the letter and taping it to the seat. Do what works for you. Here are some ideas I used in teaching colors:

- When you dress them, say what color the clothes are.

- When you give them a bath, tell them the color of their cloth or shampoo bottle.

- Tell them what color shirt you are wearing, or that you are putting them on a pink blanket.

- Choose a color of the day and look for flowers or cars that color while you are out and about.

This is knowledge folks. Like learning to crawl before you walk. An electrical engineer must know the difference between a red and black wire, so why not start them early?

Talk to them by just telling them what you are doing. "Mommy is going to make dinner. We are having spaghetti tonight. Do you know how I make spaghetti?" "I need to clean the house today. Let's start with dusting." Infants respond to this and gain trust in you sharing information. This beginning of communication with your infant will help you get into practice as well and will carry through to their adult life. You are learning to communicate with your child, and they are learning three things:

1. How to listen.

2. Mom and Dad care about me.

3. Language: How to use words to share with others.

Whether you follow my advice or not, be intentional about showing love. Talk to your spouse about things you can do to bond with your baby and build their ability to communicate and learn for the future. Keep reading this book to gain more insight and references to help you grow along with your family. You may feel there is not a lot an infant can learn, but they are absorbing everything you provide such as kind words and the tone of your voice, comforting snuggles and reassurance, the sounds and smells of the household they will grow up in, and the interactions of those who come and go from that house. The intentionality you create today is growing the adult you will have tomorrow.

Chapter 2: Toddler
Be Consistent

"Acting or done in the same way over time… to be fair or accurate. Unchanging in nature, standard or effect over time." from Oxford Languages Dictionary

The terrible twos. We've all heard about this phase, but I have to admit that I thought the 3's were worse. Two- and three-year-olds are also absolutely adorable and learning like sponges. For me, the key to surviving the toddler years was creativity and consistency. They are testing you on every front, learning boundaries, knowing how to get you to respond to them, and discovering how much they can control their environment. You must discuss these boundaries with your spouse and all those who care for your children, and STICK TO IT! Consistency in the toddler years is the single most important task to helping you stay sane. And this consistency is key in creating a kind, respectful and responsible adult.

My older two children are 20 months apart, so my daughter was quite young when we moved her into a toddler bed. As we were trying to teach her to stay in her room when she went to bed, it became a problem. We preferred not to shut the door and had a gate instead. She detested this being closed and would scream. We told her, "If you stay in your bed, we will leave the gate open. But if you get out of bed and leave your room, we will close the gate." Of course she tested this.

Not five minutes after bedtime, she pitter-pattered into the living room with an apprehensive look and sly grin as if to say, "Are you going to do anything?"

My husband kindly scooped her up, took her to her bed and repeated the rule. "Noel, we told you if you left your room, we would close the gate. So Daddy is going to close the gate."

She ran after him and stood there screaming with her arms in the air for him to pick her up. I could not tolerate the sadness of her wails and went to the garage where I sat inside the car and played some calming music. I knew she was not in danger. She was not being harmed. There was nothing wrong with her learning to stay in bed, but it was not easy. After about 10-15 minutes, Jay told her he would open the gate if she went back to bed. She returned to bed, he sang her a song and she stayed put…for that night. It took about a week of this repeated behavior for her to eventually accept the fact that we would not give in, and her screaming would not change the outcome. Consistency: Not easy, but so worth it!

Funny thing regarding this story. In recent years, as our kids were asking about how we handled specific things growing up, we told her about how she liked to get out of bed and we put the gate on her door. She said, "Oh my gosh, I remember when you did that and I would stand there saying, 'Let me out, let me out.'" But she was not talking yet, so we did not hear any words. All we heard were whines and cries. In her little mind, she was forming the words. So, our explanation to her as to why we would not let her out and how she needed to learn to fall asleep on her own, was received, even at two years old. Don't underestimate what your little ones can absorb!

Bonding

The toddler years were one of my favorite stages for bonding with my kids. They soak up everything so quickly, their vocabulary is exploding each day, and they are eager to learn and grow. Much of what I discuss in the building section of this chapter also creates a bond. It is a parent/child and teacher/pupil relationship. When your kids start playing, it is an opportunity for most parents to remember toys and games from their own childhood. Rolling a ball back and forth or pushing a car across a hard surface to one another may not seem like much, but that simple interaction is key in showing your children that they are important. The attention span is short for this age group, so you will not be stuck there for hours on end. My husband used to do puppet shows for our kids on occasion and they all had these little stools they would sit on. He would make up silly voices and funny stories to have the puppets interact. They lasted only a few minutes, but the joy and interaction of these spontaneous moments are what allowed us to have a strong influence as they got older. A wise friend once told me, "If you want a child's respect as a teen, you must gain it as a toddler". A parent can't expect their teenage daughter to value their opinion of her attire if they never interacted with her much when she was younger.

Books are wonderful to read, but even more fun to act out. Nursery rhymes can easily become a charade.

Two of our favorites, which always brought energy and laughter were "Three Little Pigs" and "Bear Hunt". Each required a bit of prep work in making the houses for the pigs or determining where each obstacle of the bear hunt would be, but it was a family affair. And Dad was always the adversary. I'm not sure if he made a better wolf or bear, but I do remember one bear hunt where we ran to our final safe place breathing heavy and laughing when the bear suddenly growled. Quinn threw the blanket back and squealed delightedly, "quick through the grass!" and we all followed going through the obstacles in reverse order. Priceless, bonding moments are sure to be had when you open the door to imagination and creativity. Building forts and playing with boxes can consume hours of time.

Okay, we have all witnessed it. A toddler having a breakdown in public. Most often this is at a store and is preceded by a parent or caregiver say, "no, you can't have that." Folks, the answer to quieting a toddler is not to give in. If they are loud, causing a scene, and you are embarrassed, it should only happen once (or limited times for those kids who are more willful). When it happens, you refuse to give in, leave the store, no matter how much you needed something, and take charge by letting the toddler know this type of behavior…

- Is not acceptable.

- Is not tolerated.

- Will not result in a positive reinforcement.

You need to enforce appropriate discipline in that moment (no video for the car ride home, time out before you drive off, a stern talking to), whatever works best for your toddler to receive the message. If this is the result of screaming in the store when you do not get a toy or treat, they will soon learn that this is not an outcome they want, and the behavior will stop. Gaining your child's respect and teaching them boundaries is a way of bonding. They gain understanding of your expectations and the rules of the household. It connects them to you and their ability to follow the rules creates a bond.

Spanking is a heated debate among parents and scholars alike. You and your spouse need to decide what discipline is acceptable for your household. If anger is an issue and there is a temptation to strike a child out of frustration and anger, you should avoid spanking. For me, spanking was a way of sending a clear message and was rarely needed. Examples of when I did spank would be running out in the street - they were taught this was not okay and very dangerous but, as I mentioned earlier, they are testing rules and boundaries. This is clearly a situation where their life is in danger, and ignoring parental authority and thinking it is funny to run away from mommy could be life threatening. If any of my children ran into harm's way after being told not to, it was an immediate swat to send the message "this is not acceptable."

In response to repeated negative behavior I would tell them, "That is not okay, and if you do it again, you will get a spanking." Of course, children will test this theory and you MUST follow through. Never give a warning unless you are prepared to do so. It is confusing for the child and negates any progress in discipline and understanding of the rules. Consistency is key!

In our household spanking created the desired results and was a rare occurrence. It should NEVER be done in anger, or repeatedly. One, firm swat sends the message. You may ponder how that is bonding. I strongly feel that creating boundaries brings understanding and respect to both parent and child in a relationship. Discipline is a form of communication. If too extreme it can build resentment. If too lenient, it shows a lack of concern. Discipline, when done consistently and fairly, bonds you together as a family.

Positive physical touch is still important. Just like those little massages for your infant; hugs, high fives, holding hands and gentle rough housing are all positive interactions that give your children security, make them feel loved, and teach them that they are valued. I used to give my son a massage on his hand and wrist during the sermon on Sunday. I did this one week when he was being exceptionally disruptive to his younger sister, and it became a routine. Sometimes he would massage mine in return. A few years later we would discover that physical touch was his top love language (from *Five Love Languages of Children* by Gary Smalley). I will share more on this in chapter five. Bonding comes in a variety of ways and should happen naturally when you spend time together and strive to get to know your child.

Begin an evening and bedtime routine. All the excitement and learning from the day makes children's minds and bodies tired come evening. Following rules is more challenging as parents are tired too. Having a routine makes it easier on everyone. Whether you stay home and the routine is cleaning up the toys from the day, or you return from day care and let them relax to enjoy their own toys for a bit, work in a daily activity they can do while you cook or help prepare the meal. You could also invite them to help. Kids are capable of more than you think. I guarantee, if you stick to the routine when you are exhausted, and while they are young, it will only get easier.

For us, it started about 30 minutes before Dad came home and when I had run out of steam and ideas to entertain them, "Let's clean up our toys." We typically played music and sometimes I would let them choose which room or items to do first. They were much more enthusiastic about helping if they felt they had some choice in the matter. (This builds on decision making and confidence). When the house was orderly, they would help me set the table or at least carry non-breakable items to the table. Greeting Dad at the door brought a few moments of reprieve for me to finish up cooking. After dinner, we had baths, some play time and watched a short video (Winnie The Pooh and Veggie Tales were among our favorites). We would read a book and tuck them in bed. They knew this would happen every night. It gave them confidence to know when the video ended, it was time to read, and after we read the lights went out and they were to stay in bed and fall asleep. The expected routine brought comfort and peace to all of us. We bonded over books, videos and nighttime routines. We still occasionally sing a "Silly Song With Larry" (*Veggie Tales*) when something strikes us.

Building

What can you do during the toddler years to build on your child's future? Part of being intentional is asking yourself questions like this. What skills do they need to find success in this world? Reading is vital. You can learn about anything if you can read. Letters of the alphabet are everywhere, and typically cheap. Magnetic letters to place on the fridge or washing machine are great to entertain your little one while you work. The bright colors and letters are easy to point out to them as they pick them up. Place simple words like "cat" together on the magnetic background and when they show interest, trade the letters to make other words…hat, fat, pat, etc. They are learning that our language has patterns and the letters have sounds. If they put together a word and ask, "Momma, what does that say?" Sound it out, even if it makes no logical sense. Laugh at their creation, but don't berate them for creating something that is not in the dictionary. Be thankful they are trying to understand these new shapes and the sounds that are connected to them. Proper spelling will come, but you are simply building the foundation of a desire to learn. Bright, colorful letters can also be found for bath time, in puzzles, card games and more. Put their language in their hands, repeat the sounds as you play with them, and watch their vocabulary and budding minds grow!

Aside from reading, you can teach basic information on any subject with common items around you. Counting anything: sidewalk squares, telephone poles, the number of red cars you see, how many people are in a room, etc. Use blocks to show how 4 make a square. $1 + 1$ is 2, and $2 + 2 = 4$. Teach science by using two ice cubes. Place one in a cup inside the house, and one outside the house. Depending on the time of year, which one melts faster and why? Look up information about basic science experiments and see how creative they become in wanting to make their own discoveries. This can apply to any topic or subject: music, biology, architecture, etc. I knew a five-year-old who could identify the make and model of nearly any vehicle. His father would point these out any time they rode together. It not only entertained the child but built up knowledge and created a bond and mutual interest. Don't underestimate the capacity your toddler has to learn. Use common, everyday experiences to help them become more knowledgeable. Allow them to play to learn how to problem solve. You are building a bright future with a wide-open door of opportunities.

Of course there are times when watching a television show or movie is appropriate, but make sure you balance screen time with non-screen. This was a rule in our house and on road trips: one hour on the screen, two hours off the screen. Sometimes the battles ensued when the timer dinged to end screen time. But on the other hand, I never had to set a timer to end their creative, imaginative play that took place off the screen. Once they got submerged into playing with trains, dolls, pretending to be a dog, or running around outside, they were having too much fun to think "I want to watch a movie." Their minds and bodies grow so much by imaginative play. Too many children are unable to problem solve today because they grew up watching other people live on a screen and did not get out and experience the hands-on discoveries of trial and error on their own.

From a relational perspective, toddler years are key in how children learn to interact with others. Sharing can be tough to learn, but very, very important. Some will cry when told to share their toys. Some become angry, and some will throw a fit or even become aggressive. Be intentional and be prepared for how you want to respond to your child and instill the quality of kindness in being able to share. Consequently, remember that you need to teach your child how to be the one who receives. What

I mean is, you also need to teach them how to be grateful and understanding to others when they share toys or food with your children. "That was very nice that Logan shared his ball with you. Can you say, 'thank you?'" Believe it or not, even little ones can grasp that they want to treat others how they like to be treated. I have seen many times over, a reluctant hand, coerced by a parent, reaching out to share a toy, then a look of surprised glee when the friend smiles and says, "thank you" in return. It ignites something in most children to make them want to share more. Seeing other people's positive responses to our gestures makes us feel pleased. Toddlers can learn this, but only if you show them.

Finally, teach them how to respect both their property and that of others. Make them clean their toys up at the end of the day. Although I do admit that some creations are worth leaving for tomorrow (villages of little people houses, books strategically laid out to represent cages in their zoo, and more elaborate imaginary worlds they created as they grew) cleaning up each day teaches responsibility, general tidiness and respect for the space around them. More importantly, when you are at another house, make sure they help their friend clean up before leaving.

Anytime they make a mess (eating a snack, changing clothes, even reading many books and laying them on the floor) show them how to clean up. DON'T DO THE CLEANING FOR THEM! This teaches them nothing except that someone else will do their dirty work. My son went through the most irritating routine of pulling all the little chunky, board books off the shelf (which was there so his sister could access and read them too) when he was about 18 months old. I do not know why this brought him such glee, but every few days, there he would be, surrounded by his pile of books. I let him play and flip through them, then watched for him to prepare for his next journey and said, "Quinn, we need to put the books back." He would hand them to me, and I would put them on the shelf. I tried to be strategic and catch him approaching the shelf when I would say, "Would you like to read a book? Let's just take one book off the shelf." Sometimes it worked, sometimes it did not, but eventually, he quit flinging the shelf empty of its contents and learned to read one at a time. I believe his wife would attest that, for the most part, he is pretty good at picking up after himself when he makes a mess.

Even the simplest of daily tasks are laying a foundation your children can build upon for the rest of their lives. Be intentional in the little things. Teach them kindness by being kind. Help them learn to laugh by laughing with them. Share your faith that they too may believe. Each child is different, so our parenting needs to be different. But we can all be intentional about how we want things to proceed for the future. Remember this when you are tired and feel doing things for them would be easier in the moment. Parenting moments are important, because they are not just about now. They are about the future of our children. Build the foundation for their strong tower of tomorrow.

Chapter 3: Pre-School
Be Instructive

"The meaning of INSTRUCTIVE is carrying a lesson: enlightening." - Merriam-Webster Dictionary

Most of us have been a part of a sports team or group who had some sort of coach. Therefore, most of us have experienced good coaches and bad coaches. A good coach is instructive: teaches us new skills, helps us see where we can improve, and motivates us by presenting achievable challenges. A bad coach makes demands, is impatient with progress, does not know how to motivate us, and any improvements made by the athletes are often done begrudgingly. Parents, you are the life coach of your children, and you have a couple decades of coaching ahead of you. Start processing now how you can be a good coach and enlighten your team. Begrudging improvements are deal breakers through the teen years. Get down on the floor and start instructing your preschooler. You'll become a champion parent and there is no greater title!

Bonding

Bonding with preschoolers can be very delightful. Their language is exploding, and their ability to understand jokes and emotions makes their unique personalities really start to shine. This is when board games can begin; and what a wonderful world of entertainment they provide. *Candy Land* is always a great early game. I find it utterly amazing to see the reaction of kids when they draw the candy cane toward the end of the game. Are they so competitive that they have a complete meltdown? Or perhaps they quietly sulk hoping no one will see their disappointment? Maybe they really don't care and are glad that the game can essentially start over for them. Your response to losing or facing a set-back will greatly influence their reaction. Why not teach them to laugh if they have to move back a few colors? Please, please, please, DO NOT change the rules or pretend the card was in the wrong place, or try to cheat so they can be happy. Folks, the gumdrop card when you are at the gingerbread house is a minor issue in life. It is a lesson that things won't always go your way. It is an opportunity to learn how to handle disappointment. There is a message of humility in learning how to be content when someone else gets something you want. To win the game is fun, but to play the game is where the joy truly lies. Teach that lesson to your preschooler and they will be much more equipped to handle being cut from a sports team, or not getting a part in a play. We must, as parents, teach our children how to navigate life. A board game may seem like a simple moment of play, but a lot of life lessons can grow from those simple moments together.

Chalk tracks was one of our great consumers of time. What, you may ask, are chalk tracks? Well, I would take two, fat pieces of chalk (one in each hand) and start at the edge of the sidewalk. Then proceed to walk backwards zig zagging across the driveway, occasionally lifting the chalk to create a break and then I would go back and make more tracks connecting the breaks so we had a whole driveway of pathways. These could be walked through with a baby carriage, driven by a tricycle, or the all-time favorite was a scooter. They were a little older when they got scooters, but they eventually added stop signs, stores off to the side, a school, and even their cousin's house (all imaginative of course). Our neighbor sometimes served as the police officer and would give a ticket if they did not stop at the sign, were driving too fast, or did not park their vehicle in the appropriate place. I have to admit that making the track was not always an easy task, but generally took 20-30 minutes for a good one, and it could result in hours and multiple days of fun. Dad had to park in the street sometimes so as not to disrupt evening play. My youngest expressed to me that this is what taught her to stay between the lines. If she rode randomly, her older siblings would fuss saying, "No, Rachel, you have to stay between the lines." She said it even helped her to do better at coloring and staying in the lines on her page. You can't predict the depth of insight simple games and natural play can bring. Be creative and see what it sparks in the imagination of your children.

I created a game for learning to tie shoes out of desperation during a long stint of horrible weather. My oldest was just on the cusp of mastering this skill and the others still needed to learn. I was surrounded by a mountain of laundry and the empty baskets gave me an idea. "Let's go fishing!" I declared (a good alternative to laundry). Quizzical and excited looks were exchanged. I said, "each of you grab a basket. This will be your fishing boat. I am going to look for poles and you go gather our fish. I want you to get all the shoes from your closet and bring them to this room."

Off they went, anxious to see how this was going to work out. I got a couple of yard sticks and a broom handle from the garage (one that unscrews, not a broken end) and we all returned to create our adventure. They spread their laundry baskets around the room, and I spread the shoes all over the floor. They had to use the stick or pole to scoop up the shoes and put them in their basket. Whenever they got a shoe with laces, they practiced tying it. For the two-year-old, she simply tucked the laces inside the shoe but wanted to feel like she had a task as well. They had so much fun that without prompting, once all the fish were caught, they dumped them out, spread them around and began again. But this time, they wanted to include Mom and Dad's shoes as well. Unfortunately, a yardstick broke trying to haul in one of Dad's "big fish" but then my son found a bungee cord with a plastic hook on the end and discovered that it made a better pole for our prey. This spontaneous game brought many hours of entertainment, and we did it on several occasions. By the time you gather shoes, play the game, then put all the shoes away, it occupies a lot of time. The kids even began to grab the sides of their basket and hop across the floor to get closer to some of the shoes. Not only did it increase their learning for tying shoes, but it also taught problem solving in how to hook the shoe on their pole and it developed their gross motor skills.

Be creative and be okay with crazy messes sometimes. Blanket forts, picnics inside, cardboard box mazes, let the creativity flow! They will create great memories and deep bonds that last a lifetime.

Sports begin around this age. This again, is an area of debate as to when kids should start playing competitively and how intensely involved you want to be. I can only offer my perspective and experiences on things. There are many other great scenarios so, as I suggested in the beginning of the book, do what is right for you and most importantly, what is right for your child. Let them play an active part in choosing what activities they want to be involved in. Just because you loved soccer and played for 14 years does not mean your child will want to do the same.

My dad set a very good example in exposing us to many things when we were young. He said he never wanted us to be invited to do something and not go because we were scared to try or did not know how to do it. It served my sisters and I well, and I tried to do the same for my kids. My kids did soccer, baseball, ice skating, football, dance, cheerleading, gymnastics, swimming, diving and track. Yep, we tried a lot of things, and I never let them quit mid-season. When they signed up for something, they owed it to their team to see it through to the end. This is a lesson of responsibility. But if they tried it and did not like it, they did not have to sign up the next season. Some we did for multiple years. Some were one and done. Gymnastics was the first that brought us to a "do we or don't we" in deciding whether or not to keep pushing.

Our son performed especially well in a couple of categories, and they approached us about wanting to put him on a team. I believe he was six at the time. He definitely had the build for it, and we were rather excited about this. But it was a significant financial commitment. I asked about uniform cost, tournament fees, travel requirements etc. My husband and I talked and prayed as a couple about what we should do, then we went to our son. "Do you like gymnastics?" we asked.

"Yes," he replied.

"What is your favorite thing about it?" we inquired.

"I really like jumping in the pit and bouncing on the trampoline" he said. (Neither of which were involved in the areas where they wanted him to compete).

"Would you like to go there two times a week instead of one?"

"No, I like being able to play with my friends at home too."

"You know you did very well on the rings and pommel horse. They would like you to learn new things on this and maybe join the team."

"I don't really want to learn more. I just like having fun when we go and jumping in the pit."

So my husband and I talked about this. I said, "I never see him practice anything he learns at gymnastics when he is home. If he was passionate about it, I would think he would want to do it at home too." We calculated the cost of him joining the team and discovered it would be a minimum of $10,000 before he reached middle school. With his lack of enthusiasm and that type of investment, we declined the offer to be on the team. We did a few more seasons "for fun", but it eventually was overshadowed by other interests and there were never any regrets for having said, "no" to that particular opportunity. Just because your child shows aptitude does not mean they have to pursue that avenue. I feel the openness of our conversations and the fact that we did not force them to stick with something they were not enjoying created a mutual respect and deepened the bond between us.

I mentioned how discipline can be a part of bonding in the first chapter and I want to expand on that here. Having clear guidelines results in mutual respect and understanding. In this effort to create guidelines, there are inevitable moments of having to tell your children "No", and to discipline them.

As previously discussed, my son's love language is physical touch. (I highly recommend you read Gary Smalley's book, *The Five Love Languages for Children*. He describes how different forms of discipline will be more effective depending on what love language is important to your child.) In Quinn's case, spanking was effective because physical touch is his primary love language. If a child's love language is quality time, then being sent to their room alone is a hard pill to swallow (as opposed to an introvert who loves being by themselves). And one whose primary love language is words of affirmation would be suitably disciplined with a firm scolding. My grandmother, Eble, was known for saying, "I treat you different because you are different," in reference to raising her five children. Even if you only have two children, they are different. What works for one may not work for the other. The best way to understand their differences is spending time with them. Here are ways that I found to help build skills while also gaining insight into their individual personalities.

Building

Cooking, chores and finances are all topics you can begin building upon in this phase of your child's life. Food is an essential part of our lives, and teaching your children how to cook food is a great gift. I must admit my intentions of having my kids enjoy learning to cook were much greater than my actual achievement in this matter, likely because I myself have never enjoyed cooking. On occasion, yes, it is great to see everyone working together and having fun in the kitchen, but trying new recipes, mixing different spices, and tasting new cuisine is simply not something I enjoy. However, we rarely ate out due to the expense, and we always enjoyed our time around the table as a family without the interruption of wait staff or distraction of others in a restaurant. I have several dishes I cook very well, and I started teaching my kids to make these when they were young. What can you teach a four-year-old in the kitchen?

- The names of ingredients and what they do.

- The difference between fruits and vegetables.

- The names of various utensils and how they are used for cooking.

Simply standing on a stool and dumping ingredients into a bowl while I measured the proper amounts was thrilling for my kids. I have photos of them standing on a chair making cookies and wearing little aprons my mother made. Teaching life skills is time consuming, mentally taxing, and less enjoyable for the cook to have to focus on little hands and many questions while preparing a meal, but once again, the brief challenging moments are fleeting and produce results beyond expectation.

By age four children can begin to learn responsibility and as such they gain confidence, feel a stronger sense of belonging and have an important place in their family and in the world as a whole. We all have a desire to be needed, and when a child learns that they are capable of accomplishing things, they realize they are valued and needed. So how does one go about teaching responsibility? Chores. This will be different for each of you depending on your environment, what works well for your organizational skills and how comfortable you may be. Please do not take my advice based on what I did as the only way to proceed on everything. These are suggestions and ideas based on what worked for me. Each family and each child is unique.

I remember the exact moment when I realized my oldest child was capable of doing something on her own which I had consistently done for her. "Momma, I want a drink." Whether or not she had said "please" is not seared in my memory, but I'm sure I would have suggested she add that to her request as that would be instructive. Nonetheless, we had just purchased a refrigerator with the ice and water on the exterior and she was tall enough to reach it. I promptly got a plastic cup and taught her how to get water for herself. She was quite impressed by her skills and asked if either of her siblings was thirsty. Needless to say, by the next morning all of their plastic cups, plates and utensils were placed in a cabinet at their level so even getting her own dinnerware was achievable. Bingo! One less thing Mom has to do. I thought, *"What else is she capable of doing?"*

Our chore chart was a wooden plaque with white, round tags that hung on nails. Having three kids, I decided to create three tasks in each of the following categories: Kitchen (set table, clear table, unload dishwasher), Household (recycling, sort laundry, take out trash) and Cleaning (dust, vacuum, clean kids' bathroom). These were rotated weekly so one kid did not get stuck doing the same thing all the time. As you can see, the kitchen chores were more daily whereas the cleaning was once a week and household as needed. Now here is the challenge with requesting a four-year-old to unload the dishwasher. You have to be diligent about removing sharp knives or large items they can't manage. My kids had a spot on the counter where they sat items from the really high shelves. The first time my son put the silverware away, it was all in the right drawer, and that was about it. But I did not come after him and redo it. This would negate the entire reason for giving them a chore. It would say, "You are not good enough, your time does not matter, I don't approve of your work." A better way is to thank them for the job they did, tolerate a bit of a search for a couple days, then next time, show them how to do it better.

Another example of how to teach appropriate chores for this age would be in dusting. Little ones need to be taught how to remove special items, dust the shelf, dust the fancy items, then put them back on the shelf. If you never show them the proper way to dust, don't expect them to do it correctly. And like all things, it takes time. You don't become proficient at writing letters the first time you learn to pen them. It takes time, practice, and a lot of patience from the teacher. But my friends let me tell you, being patient and dealing with blotchy mounds of dust or forks in the spoon section are temporary. The rewards of such inconveniences are beyond what you can imagine! It results in teenagers who have confidence. They grow into young adults who know how to manage a household and share in the workload of a busy family, not to mention the respect they gain for you because you took time to teach them. That patience when they put a red sock in the light colors and explained to them why dark colors have to be washed in cold water will pay off. Tolerating growth is very different from stunting growth. Believe along with them. Expect them to improve and they will expect the same of themselves.

Paid opportunities for extra chores is something we introduced toward the end of this pre-school phase. I believe they were five or six when they first got an allowance, and it was very small. I'm thinking $1 or $2 per week. Mind you, this would have been the turn of the 21st century, so I think $5 today would be generous for this age. I can actually understand arguments for or against an allowance. Should they receive money for doing the regular chores which everyone in the family has to participate in simply because they are part of the family and have the opportunity to live where they do? That is a decision you and your spouse need to agree on. Part of choosing to give an allowance is also instructing them on how to spend it wisely. Don't just give them money and not teach them how to manage it.

When I speak of paid opportunities, I want to explain what I mean beyond those triple chores which were non-negotiable each week. A paid opportunity typically occurred because they wanted to buy something. "Can I get a new toy?" Instead of just giving it to them or having them ask grandma next time she was around, I added some non-essential tasks to the bottom of the chore chart and assigned a dollar amount to those items based on how long they would take to accomplish. At this young age, I added things like: dust all the baseboards, dust windowsills, water the plants, sweep the tile floors, collect hangers and bring them to the laundry room, etc. Let me tell you, this was a great way to get things done as they grew older. Wash the car, clean the windows, empty and wipe out kitchen cabinets were among some of my better paid opportunities. I would encourage you to think practically. When your child is an adult and they want something, is someone just going to give it to them? No, they will have to earn it. So go ahead and teach them how to do that now. The world will be much less confusing and surprising if they gain an understanding of how it works while they still live under your roof.

These examples of how to build your children up in the kitchen, do household chores and understand money management are the start of growing independent, confident adults. Walk beside them in the journey of learning how to be responsible. Show me a five-year-old who was taught how to get a wet paper towel to pick up the crumbs left behind after you sweep into a dustpan, and I will show you a child who feels content with who they are as a person and who knows, in that moment, that they have a purpose. Be content with the purpose your child has for your family in each phase of their life. Learn to be content with your purpose as a parent in that phase. Your empty nest will not be such a scary thought if you all prepare for that journey as you pass through each phase. It will be a welcomed wonder to watch them fly.

Chapter 4: Elementary
Be Involved

"Taking part in something; being part of something or connected with something."
from Oxford Learners Dictionary

When your children begin to spread their wings and explore life outside of "the nest", it is important for you to be involved and stay aware of their environment. This can be a challenge for some parents who still want control of the environment. Being involved is participating, being associated or connected to, *not controlling*. The teachers and administrators are the ones in charge, and we become involved to understand the new world of our children. Go on a field trip, help out in the classroom, coach a team, those are all great ways to be involved, but remember to give your child space and freedom as you connect to their world on the peripherals.

I can still picture the first morning our oldest daughter got on the bus. Her dad was going to take her, but she wanted to ride the bus to school. She proudly wore her new backpack full of folders, crayons, pencils and notepaper and she could not have been more excited. Her siblings, still in their pajamas, sat on the steps of the porch and watched her leave. She waved from the bus window and the two little ones ran to the end of the driveway and waved until the bus was out of sight. My husband, who worked near the kindergarten building, followed the bus and watched her walk inside. Her first major rite of passage and independent adventure had come. How do we prepare our kids and ourselves for success through this separation?

Bonding

Naturally, we all want to protect our children from harm. We bundle them up when it is cold outside. We hold their hand to cross a street. We feed them good food to stay healthy. We don't let them watch violent shows on television. We lock the doors in our house and watch over them when they play outside. All of these things are good parenting skills and important to keep your child safe. But how do we protect them when they are away from us, and how do we prepare them to protect themselves?

Remember that I have no degree in child psychology. I am simply a mother with three successful adult children. My way of doing things is not the only way, and each of you has to make choices that are best for your children. In the following pages I share things that were successful for my household. Communication comes easily for me. I grew up in a home where both parents talked to us about life issues fairly openly. My top strength from Don Clifton's *Strengths Finder* is communication. If this is not a natural tendency for you, I encourage you to step out of your comfort zone and work at speaking more directly with your kids. We talked about dangers in the world such as, "If anyone ever approaches you and tries to get you to come to their car or asks directions, just run away."

"Why Momma?" they would ask.

"Because, although most people in the world are good, there are a few who are not, and they might think you are very cute and smart and want to take you to their home."

Of course, this will be alarming to a child, but sharing the information and helping them be aware is better than never speaking of it and leaving them naive and vulnerable. You don't have to get over dramatic and grab them by the shoulders or be forceful with your description telling them a stranger could want to kill them. That would be too much and could cause great fear. The thought of being taken away from you and their home is enough for them to be aware. Bring it up on occasion, not weekly or daily. These open dialogues of sharing about the world and preparing them to live in it create trust and continue to build the bond between you.

Help your child to memorize their address and phone number. Most kindergarteners do this anyway, but we were delighted to discover that you can take nearly any address and put it to the tune of *"Rain, Rain, Go Away"*:

> *"My name's Marcia Smith, this is my address: 000 Nothing Lane, Superficial, State."*

Thank you to Noel's kindergarten teacher, who introduced us to this. It worked for anyone whose name I tried. Memorizing our phone number was a bit trickier, but we just slowly worked on the groups of numbers until they had it down. Because his office was so close to the school, we also had them memorize the name of their dad's company and what department he worked in. Make a plan and be intentional about seeing it through.

These are all ways to protect them, but how do you prepare them? There are many aspects of preparation for the world around them. One is by giving them knowledge. General information like knowing the alphabet, how to count and helping them learn to read is a good start. We had a phonics game which taught letter sounds, kept a chart of the alphabet in their room, and passed time in the car or standing in line by counting things. Take moments during the natural flow of your day to help them learn things that will be a part of their future. This is the common sense aspect of parenting. Don't set your child in front of a screen with cartoons or games all day and expect them to become a productive member of society. And don't treat them like a Harvard Law Student doing nothing but formal lectures and bombardment of information. When you make learning life skills fun, playful, and part of their daily routine, you all bond along the way.

- Teach them how to pick out outfits and dress themselves by reviewing the weather and learning how to match colors.

- Play a game of cards where you have to say the sound of the letter on the card you pick up (cards with the alphabet of course).

- Draw a map of the neighborhood and have them fill in the names of the street to understand where they live.

- Talk about fruits and vegetables while you walk through the store and what nutrients are in different colors, or why those are important to eat.

This is how you prepare your children to be in the world. You teach them about the world which brings understanding and knowledge. It often evokes an inner desire to learn more: a growing curiosity inside them.

How do you prepare children to interact with others? This one is going to depend a great deal on you because you have to understand your child and their natural tendencies in crowds as well as providing opportunities for them to be around others. Although I have read no studies on the matter yet, it seems natural that Covid isolation would have delayed social development in young people. Even if they were out and about, not being able to see people's smiles or facial reactions to stimuli would prevent the opportunity to learn from observing those reactions.

When you take your child to a park, they learn that they might have to wait their turn for a swing or be in line to go down the slide. You help them to be kind to others as they pass by and to not push someone off the beam as they walk along it. If you have friends and neighbors over to play, your child learns to share their toys, help a friend clean up before they leave, and to thank people when they give them something or do a task for them.

Parents: MANNERS ARE IMPORTANT! I think it is a bit neglected these days, but you are responsible to teach your children manners and manners matter! Do we not notice a young person who stops to hold the door vs. one who walks through without ever looking back? Have you ever passed out information to a group of people and taken note of the two or three who said, "Thank you"? Mom and Dad, it is up to you to teach these things, and you need to start when they are young, but remind them of this each day they leave for school.

- Be kind to others

- Take turns

- Use your manner words

- Please

- Thank you

- Yes ma'am

- No sir

The teachers will notice, and friends will be easier for them to find if your children have confidence and a kind character. Think of intentional ways to be consistent and stay involved in all opportunities to instill manners. Mimicking them yourself is the best teacher of all.

Choosing friends is another very important aspect of going to school. How do you encourage your kids to choose good friends? I used to tell my kids to be friends with people who treat others with kindness. If someone is always whispering about other people or making fun of them, that is not kind. If a child is rude or mean to others, they are likely going to be mean and rude to their friends as well. And I am going to share the advice my mother-in-law gave to her son when they moved to a new town. He inquired, "Mom, how do I make friends?"

She wisely told him, "Ask them questions. People like to share stories about themselves, so if you ask them questions, they will enjoy talking and you can learn what things you have in common."

I encourage you to tell your children to ask questions of others. For a six-year-old, things like

- Do you have any pets?

- Do you have any brothers or sisters?

- What do you like to play outside?

These are all great conversation starters for young people. If you have a particularly shy child, have them learn one question and encourage them to ask kids who sit next to them. It might bring them some confidence if they have that prepared question they know they can use and do not have to be nervous about what to do if someone new is beside them.

One more aspect of preparedness is regarding natural disasters such as a storm or fire. I think it is good to have these conversations before they go to school, so the teacher is not the first to mention it. I can tell you, your parent rating goes way up if you have already talked to your kids about something the teacher tells them. They automatically think the teacher is smart, and when you know something the teacher knows, you are even smarter!

Our oldest daughter, for some reason, hated to talk about fire. To this day, she cannot tell us why it made her sad, but she used to cover her ears if I said the word, "fire." Nonetheless we practiced a fire drill at home. I told her it was better to practice and never have to use it, than to have a fire and not know how to react or what to do. This seemed to calm her nerves a bit, but she still detested our conversations and walkthroughs of fire escape routes. When I told her she should go into her sister's room if the stairs are blocked and open the window and she would be able to climb onto the roof and someone would be below. With a shocked look and hands on her hips she declared, "And you want me to jump?" Thankfully we never had a fire, but the conversation had happened, and she would have been prepared.

Sharing information about the realities of life will prepare your child to handle life situations. The common sense in this is to do it naturally. Speaking of horrible situations where people were burned alive only creates fear, not preparedness. Protect your children, yes. But prepare them. I believe each household is going to approach this differently depending on your own experiences in life, where you live, and the environment your kids will face in the real world. But plan ahead, process what they need to know, and the best way to communicate. Be intentional, be consistent, and teach what is appropriate for their age.

Family dinners were one of the single most important ways that our family bonded. The amount of communication, laughter, bantering, and disagreements shared over a meal at the Endicott household can't be calculated. Parents and siblings get to hear about one another's days and children gain understanding about what their parents do at work. We talked about life issues, politics, and slang words. Bond together over food. It is a very filling activity!

I shared about our bedtime routine when the kids were younger and reading before bed continued through these years. The new part of this was having the kids read to us or gathering for stories as a family. The *Junie B. Jones'* series by Barbara Park was a favorite and I always knew when it was being read to their dad because I would hear his guffaws ring throughout the house. It is common knowledge that these books are to be kept until he is old and living in a retirement home. The kids are to come read Junie B. to him and make him laugh. Memories of reading together will be carried on through many decades. Take extra time and read with your kids tonight! Oh, and include a book in their stocking this year. It's a good tradition.

Building

We spoke about manners earlier in this chapter, but there is more to being able to make an impact on other lives than keeping a check on our own behavior. We have to teach our children how to get along with others who are quite different from themselves. Sometimes this involves learning how to tolerate poor behavior, or simply trying to understand why someone is acting a specific way. We can help our children gain social intelligence by allowing them to share stories about interactions with others and interpret how to respond or help them empathize with other people's situations.

One of my kids inquired about someone in their class who was particularly mean. "He is always rude to people or making fun of them. He says really mean stuff to purposely hurt their feelings. Why does he do that Mom?"

"Well," I said, "how do you think his parents talk to him at home? Do you think they are nice and encouraging?"

They thought for several minutes about this and replied, "You think he talks that way to kids at school because his parents talk that way to him? That makes me sad."

I suggested, "It makes me sad too. It is still not okay for him to speak like that, but the best thing you can do is probably to ignore his rude comments as much as possible and be kind when you can. Besides, most kids who are bullies do it to get attention, even if it is negative attention. If you do not respond, they grow bored and will eventually stop."

Folks, this is not the case with every situation. Some kids are so in your face, you can't ignore them or if you are kind in return they may haul off and slug you. As I said in the first chapter, my experiences and shared advice are not the end all be all, but please just stop and ponder situations your kids experience and ask yourself, "What is the best way to respond to this?" Use your personal experience and knowledge to make wise decisions with your kids!

My younger daughter told me a girl in her class seemed really sad and so she asked her if she was okay, and the girl shared that her grandparent had died over the weekend. This prompted Rachel to be especially helpful that day and to sit with her at recess listening to stories of her grandmother instead of running around with the others. Watching other people, learning to read emotions and being able to respond by stepping out of the way when someone's anger is brewing, offer kindness when someone is sad, or simply to smile at a person who seems lonely are all ways your child can gain social intelligence. This understanding and wisdom about the different circumstances people come from will help them change the focus from internal impatience and ignorance to empathy and tolerance of those differences.

As in previous chapters I want to spend a little time sharing about how to build on your student's knowledge. You are not the sole teacher anymore. And this is a good thing. We all learn differently. Some of us learn by listening, some by watching and some by doing. Having a variety of teachers means more opportunities for your kids to learn in different ways. Whatever your children are learning at school should be built upon at home.

I especially enjoyed playing with coins and helping them count at home. A great winter game can be made by saving the empty boxes and jars of some of your favorite foods. Simply stick them in a box in the garage or bag in the closet for a rainy or cold, snowy day. Have your kids write prices on them and set up a make-believe store. For younger children, they can buy one item at a time. For older kids, they can learn to add items together and count out the exact change. You can even practice multiplication and explain taxes if they are ready for that step.

You know how I encouraged you to use life situations as learning opportunities? Think of how you could use this to help them plan a healthy meal. Ask them to purchase something from each food group to pretend they are going to cook for their family. Practice reading by showing them how to read ingredients and look at the nutrients in the items they are buying. Have a generic brand and name brand of the same item and compare the two. Often the same company makes both products, but one gets the advertised label. The stuff inside is the same, but greatly discounted on the generic brand. All these little tricks, that take a bit of time now, are building knowledge and real-world skills which will produce informed, independent, confident adults.

Build on those reading and writing skills by teaching them the importance of correspondence, specifically thank you notes! A hand-written thank you note is still common courtesy and people notice. If your child can write their name, they can write a thank you note. A simple, "Dear Grandma, thank you for the birthday money. I love you, Christine." That is sufficient for a 1st grader and by 5th grade, they should be able to tell grandma what they intend to use the money for and share a sentence or two about why they appreciate grandma or what they love about her.

My sister recently shared a story of adult professionals tasked with writing thank you notes to a group of soldiers thanking them for their service. She was shocked by the number of them who had no idea how to do this. They eventually looked up "how to write a thank you note to a soldier." Folks, that is not acceptable for adult professionals to not know the basics of how to write a thank you note. Teach your children today! Our rule was that they were not allowed to play with a birthday toy or Christmas gift until they wrote their thank you note. We did not make them write a note to us as we lived in the same house, but external people…absolutely. It is important! It builds confidence to learn how to express gratitude and reminds them of how important it is to appreciate what others do for them in life.

When family members are spending most of the day in different environments it is natural that you will experience new opportunities and your children will hear information from other people that will bring into question some of the rules and practices you have at home. I can't tell you what incident prompted the first family meeting, but I can tell you that the words "family meeting" brought groans from all three of my children. The first one was exciting as no one knew what I was talking about. We all came together and I stood with a wooden spoon in my hand. "This is the speaking spoon. Only the person holding this spoon is allowed to speak. Everyone else has to listen. When I am done speaking you can raise your hand to receive the spoon." Blank looks and smirks were shared.

"And," my husband added, "when you take the spoon, you have to share two or three sentences about what the person before you just said before you begin talking."

Dropped jaws and eye rolls ensued. My husband and I had experienced this type of conversation with a student from Asbury Seminary who was using us as a testing couple for a conflict communication class. By repeating what the person before you says, it helps you focus on listening rather than just the retort you have in mind.

In all honesty, we did not have that many family meetings. I don't even think it was once a year. But when things in the house escalated or there were issues we wanted to address, we called a family meeting. Now, the kids laugh when we mention it and remember some key decisions coming out of those experiences. They are all newlyweds with no children yet, so I don't believe the speaking spoon has reared its head, but I'll be surprised if they do not resort to it one day. After all, our kids once called a family meeting themselves because they wanted

Mom and Dad to listen to what they had to say. This story is shared in chapter five.

All the communication we do now is building on how they will communicate in the future. Negotiating with siblings prepares them to talk openly with peers. Learning to respect the rules of their parents helps them prepare for following a boss. No time and energy you put into your kids today will be wasted as each moment prepares them for the future.

Our final discussion in the elementary years is regarding finances. Remember that I told you to not give your children an allowance or pay them for chores if you are not prepared to teach them how to manage money? Well, this is another conversation you need to have with your spouse. Typically there is one spouse who is more adept at financial planning than the other, but both of you should be aware of where you stand with money, and you should review it regularly together. Once you have children in the picture, you need to discuss how you are going to teach them and what you want to teach them. We came to a decision that our young children needed to tithe 10% of what they earned. They could choose what they wanted to give that 10% to: church, mission's group, homeless shelter, etc.... so they kept track of what they made and had a jar to keep their 10%. We also encouraged savings, and that developed more when they had more money to save.

It was not uncommon when we were at the store for my son to find something he wanted to purchase. "Mom, I don't have my money with me, but I have it at home. Can I get this toy and pay you back?" I typically agreed, and he did pay me back at home. But I realized at some point that this was teaching him two things:

- Impulse buying.

- Buying on credit.

Neither of these were things I wanted him to get into the habit of doing. So I told him, "Quinn, if you want to buy something, you will have to have your money with you." The next time it happened, he said he would go back and buy the toy but then forgot about it in a couple of days. I reminded him when we returned to the store (and were already outside again) that he had forgotten about that toy. This prompted the ability to explain impulse buying and how important it is to wait sometimes and ponder your purchase before diving in to a quick decision. He became quite frugal with his spending for a few years. Mowing and other odd jobs brought more money plus the transition from toys to more expensive items such as video games squandered his earnings rather quickly during early teen years. He managed to graduate from college debt free and is completely supporting himself. I know the ease of online shopping is a temptation, but those discussions with him in the early years helped build the habits he carries today in contemplating the true need of things before making an impulsive buy. Do not underestimate the importance of communicating about everything and sharing the good, bad, and ugly stories to help your children learn how to gain financial responsibility and independence.

The elementary age is a fabulous time for taking those early years of protection and turning them into opportunities for your children to see how prepared they are to bond with others through skills they learn in their daily routine of life. You build from those moments of understanding by helping them learn to observe and expand their relationships with others, increase communication and manage their own life. This comes by making choices in food, relationships, and finances. Increased knowledge allows for a better understanding of the world in which they live and the ability to grow into the independent adults you have been intentionally, consistently, instructing them to become.

Chapter 5: Middle School
Be Present

"Giving yourself a time where you're not focusing or doing. A time where you're just being present. The idea of being present is often associated with mindfulness. Being mindful with our thoughts means you observe them, but you don't judge them." From healthline.com: "How to be Present at Work, in Relationships and More" by Crystal Raypole

I love this explanation of being present because it is exactly what pre-teen and early teens need. Time when you are mindful with your thoughts in observing them, but not judging them. Folks, this is a challenging time. I survived my own middle school years partially because I was behind the times emotionally as well as physically (didn't blossom until my sophomore year in high school), so I was a bit oblivious to all the drama that others had. But my children were all amongst the oldest of their class and right in the mix of emotional and physical growth. They feel awkward, a need to be more independent, and a desire to prove themselves even if they don't know who they are. Because they are confused on many fronts, and bombarded by information from others, they often do not want to talk or answer questions from Mom or Dad (this was especially true with my son). So you need to glean information by being present, even if your child has no extracurriculars for you to be involved in. If you can't be present at school or in transporting them, then find ways to be present at home. Connecting as a family is key in keeping communication open and continuing to bond with one another in building the kind, productive, confident adult you have been striving for since their birth.

Bonding

It is likely I could quote more than a dozen books or podcasts which stress the importance of a family meal. I've heard about the significance of this since the 1950s when Swanson did mass marketing for TV dinners and evening television began to invade the tradition of families sitting down to eat their dinner at the table. From before our children were born, dinner together was part of the Endicott routine. It is where we connected at the end of the day, shared stories about our work experiences, discussed the happenings of the world and created short-term and long-term plans. For us, this naturally continued as we had children. Disrupted at times, yes. But the goal to all sit down together was set every day.

Having your entire household around the table together creates a bond. Make sure you disconnect from screens during this time. Television should be off and phones on silent. *Yes, Mom and Dad, even yours—especially yours.* Lead by example and show your family that for those few minutes in your day, nothing else is more important to you. Sharing the same food, stories and even dishes can sear memories into your brain that will last forever. I still become nostalgic when I smell sauerkraut, as it was a standard at my grandmother's house. I found a dish in an antique store that I recalled my mother always using to make Jell-O. I've observed my kids make jokes about the Pfaltzgraff dishes I use as half the wedding registries in the early 90s were not complete without them. All of these are examples of memories created by sharing together around a dinner table.

It is not easy with varying schedules to sit teens down to eat at the same time but work to adjust the schedule for the maximum amount of family members. Sometimes we needed to eat early because of a late practice or performance and sometimes we needed to eat late for the same reason. Often, even when one of the kids could not be home for dinner, I took it to them. This was especially true during plays and musicals.

Practices leading up to a performance were often long and late. They had a break for meals and we found a variety of solutions for feeding them. Many parents brought fast-food to their kids. And that is okay. It was part of their family traditions and bonding. Some kids used the vending machines or packed cold items from home (which mine often did as well). We lived close enough that I was occasionally able to bring them a plate from our table. At first, my daughter thought this was weird and was slightly embarrassed. But then she saw the reaction of her friends. They would nose around and ask questions about what had been prepared. Some were completely in awe that she had homemade lasagna or mashed potatoes. She discovered that although the family meal was standard in our home, it was lacking in many others. It was a first glimpse of the reality that her life and experiences were different. She began to appreciate some of the things her parents did…SOME. She's still a teenager and appreciating what other people do, especially parents, is not a function her brain concludes naturally. My point is to make every effort possible to bring your family together every day. If not dinner, try breakfast. Make them sit down, if only for 20 minutes, and share about what is happening. These moments are vital. They may bring laughter, they may result in an occasional argument, but they bring you together for the same purpose and this creates a lasting bond. It communicates that they are important, that they are part of a family, and that the family is working on the daily routine of life together.

I did not know what an insightful treasure I possessed when I volunteered to start a middle school volleyball program, but it was the year my daughter was heading to 6th grade, and I had an inside scoop on school happenings. Listening to the students as they walked into practice, hearing stories on the bus, visiting as we waited for parents to arrive and take them home, it was all insight into the world of my children.

I strongly recommend you volunteer in any capacity possible to help out with activities at school. If your child is in the band, offer to haul equipment and set-up for concerts. If your child goes to a youth group, be a chaperone and volunteer to bring snacks. If your child is in a sport, work the concession stand, sit near the bench where you can hear the other kids interact and be an involved parent who cheers and encourages, but don't be too obnoxious. Most teens do not like their parents to draw attention. Okay, maybe when it came to cross country I was a bit obnoxious, but I did cheer for everyone on the team, and some of those kids even made suggestions about tough areas of the course where they wanted me to be cheering them on. If you can't be there at school, kick a ball in the backyard, watch a team on TV and engage in conversation about good plays and good character. Support their activities but keep the balance between allowing them to enjoy it and being forced to practice all the time. Extracurricular activities should be fun and stress relieving for all of you.

I could not always provide it, but whenever possible, my husband or I would pick the kids up from school. This was prime listening time. They had just been released from a full day of soaking in information and they were ready to spit some things back out. Well, one of my kids was. The other two liked to process a bit, before sharing details, but riding in a car is a very non-threatening way for a kid to share information. You are not looking them in the eye and you are distracted with driving. They can ask hard questions. Oh my, did I get some hard questions while driving in the car! For example: What does an abortion mean? Why do some women get pregnant before they are married? What's the f-word? How do people know if they are gay? What was your biggest regret in life? What were you and Dad arguing about this morning? What does fascist mean? … and so on and so on. If that car could talk! Be present whenever possible by turning your phone off and turning your ears on. It is an incredible bond to know someone hears what you say and respects you for sharing it.

Being present at home takes years of knowledge about your child, patience in holding your tongue when you have a thousand words to say and a bit of stealth. My young teens were caught in a world between childhood and becoming adults. Toys like barbies and matchbox cars still beckoned their attention, but they were wanting to be more advanced with video game options, makeup and hairstyles. Most teens feel like they are the only individuals in the world going through the challenges that befall them. This feeling of uncertainty can create a tendency to withdraw. While it is important to allow your children privacy, we also need to protect them from the dangers that result in too much privacy. I'm not going to get into the details of setting parameters on phones and computers. What I am going to share are things that worked for us in continuing to bond with teens who wanted to withdraw.

I mentioned that knowing your kids and a bit of stealth may be needed and here is why. I had one child who loved to share information. She needed a listening ear. But she did not want advice. She point blank told me, "Mom, I don't need your opinion. I just want you to listen." I was thankful she wanted to share and listened when she needed to talk. Holding my tongue sometimes took a firm grip from my teeth and many reminders from my husband that I needed to wait until she actually asked for my opinion. This need from your teens for you to not say what you are thinking, by the way, continues into parenting adult children. Get used to it!

Okay, onto child number two. He detested questions as a teen. Even a simple greeting like, "How was your day?" or "Did you sleep well?", could elicit the most vicious retort of irritation. Choosing the battles of instilling respect and general courtesy vs. knowledge that the snarling beast of hunger needed to be fed were sometimes like walking a tightrope. But food became an open door for being present with this one. When he was in his room studying or uber focused on a video game, I could divert his attention with a fresh batch of cookies, cheese and crackers or anything peanut butter. It was not uncommon for me to deliver these to him along with my own plate. See, this was part of the stealth. If I had a plate for myself, I could sit in the room and eat mine while he would eat his own. This often created a moment where he would turn and share information with me. Instead of biting my tongue, I was simply able to stuff more food into my mouth to prevent me from offering unsolicited advice. It also provided opportunity for me to pat his back or give a shoulder squeeze to remind him how much I care. Oh, and always leave the dishes in the room when you leave. This gives an excuse to return later and offer another opportunity for them to speak.

And then there was my third child. She held everything inside. I always knew when something was bothering her, but she typically, even to this day, needed time to process. After having one daughter who immediately blasted anything and everything, it took a lot of trial and error to learn how to develop new bonding techniques with this one. In the end, it was the dog and books which offered the best solutions. The family dog, Jenna, enjoyed hanging out in her room. I wonder now if that was partially because Jenna knew Rachel needed her presence. Nonetheless, it provided an opportunity for me to go in and just sit with the dog to pet her, make-up things the dog might say (which broke the ice and brought laughter), and to wait patiently for Rachel to be ready to talk. Occasionally I would just take a book into her room. She'd ask, "What are you doing?"

I would reply, "I just thought I would sit here and read a bit." It was not always welcomed but thankfully, rarely dismissed. Inevitably, in the midst of her pretending to be focused on her studies, she would turn and start sharing all that was weighing on her mind. My presence frequently resulted in her crying on my shoulder. We had a lot of deep discussions with Jenna lying next to us. Because she had already processed through multiple scenarios in her mind, she was typically ready to hear my advice. She still calls today when she is ready to share, as do her siblings, and they know I am always willing to listen. These encounters with my children were not daily or even weekly, but I watched each of them enough to know when they seemed heavy and withdrawn. Just as you determine the varying cries of your infant, moms know when something is bothering their teen. The study of your children never ends, and using the knowledge you have of them to continue to bond and help them grow will plant the roots which result in mighty oaks who can withstand the storms of life.

You can't bond with someone when you are never around them. And when they come around you, pay attention. For this reason, we did not allow our kids to have a television in their room. When complaining one Christmas that a friend had gotten one for their room I simply said, "Well they do not live in the Endicott household. In our house, we share the television. There are too many shows that have information which is not good to watch alone. We want to laugh and share what we view. Furthermore, having a TV in your room is a temptation to watch it and not sleep. This is not a healthy habit. We are removing those temptations for you by not putting a TV in your room." They were not entirely convinced by my argument, but they never brought it up again.

We also made our children plug their phones in for the night in our bedroom. There is nothing good that can come from 24-hour access to all that these devices expose, especially in the overnight hours. Again, remove the temptation by starting from the first day they get a cell phone. You want a phone? Then you follow our rules. You must charge it in Mom and Dad's bedroom at night. No exception. Do they need an alarm and music to fall asleep? Those can be purchased for about $20 which is a small investment for removing all they can become entangled with on their electronic devices.

Have discussions with your spouse about other rules and boundaries you want to set BEFORE you purchase the phone. If you feel it is necessary, have your kid sign a contract to agree to things such as giving parents passwords to social media. Those are things I am not going into detail about, but they are very critical for intentional parenting. We only had one centrally located computer when my kids were teens, so that is another item you will need to be intentional with in regard to rules. Continue to have fun in these trying times. Whatever your family does: hiking and camping, playing board games or cards, crazy dance nights, telling stories, gaming, or movies, do it together. Laugh often. I've never heard anyone say they regret laughing too much while their kids were growing up.

Speaking of laughter, remember my insight about our family meetings in the previous chapter? We had an intriguing surprise one night when the children came to our room with a wooden spoon in hand and said, "We want to call a family meeting."

I do not remember who spoke first, but I do remember that I started to say something, and they quickly cut me off because I was not holding the speaking spoon. What it came down to was a plea to stay up one hour longer one night per week. This was during the early seasons of *American Idol* and our family, as lovers of music, greatly enjoyed this show. As the season came to a close, the night someone got voted off was a two-hour show and ran past their bedtime. We typically recorded it and watched it later. But they argued that everyone at school would spoil it for them as their friends discussed the results. They could not participate in the conversations and felt frustrated that we would not let them watch it. They used examples of how well behaved they were, that they all stayed healthy (for the most part), and they made good grades and stayed awake in class. They did not feel one day out of the week would damage this in any way. Jay and I felt these were good arguments. But more than that, we were impressed by the way they came together in a united front and respectfully asked us to see things from their perspective. We agreed, they felt empowered, and family meetings brought on a whole new meaning. In fact, this spurred us to review some of our household rules and create a new chart for the summer that everyone agreed on. It was fabulous because this was the summer I started working and the kids were often at home for several hours by themselves. They were able to be a part of deciding how to take on the new responsibilities we expected of them.

Building

I told you that our chore chart had three items in each category so they could share equally. Well, this was the case with other chores as well. When I left for work during the summer, I often wrote down a list of things I needed them to do for the day. I always wrote them in sets of three. Three, six or nine items were easy to come up with. Our son, who was an early riser, quickly learned that he could get first glance at the list and claim the three items which he deemed easiest. A "Q" was next to each thing he planned to accomplish long before his sisters woke up. Funny though, I think he was often the one running through the house ten minutes before my arrival to get his chore complete.

Responsibility brings confidence. Knowing they were expected to get something done helped them feel responsible both to me and other family members. Claiming a chore as their own was a sense of belonging and expectation. Crossing it off the list brought accomplishment and gratitude. Please give your children chores and give them consequences when they are not completed. Ignoring incomplete expectations breeds self-dissatisfaction and laziness. Teach them the joy of helping others rather than the entitlement of watching someone else perform tasks which should be their own responsibility.

I'm not sure what it is about middle school, but it seems the amount of projects is amplified such as dioramas, science fair experiments, group presentations in full costume: there were a plethora of tricky little assignments we navigated. Oh how easy it would be to just glue those little pieces for them while they slept. But would it teach them anything? Would it create a better child, a better adult for me to do the work for them? Absolutely not! *Never, ever do your kids' homework for them.* You won't be there to help them finish a report at work one day, and they need to learn how to manage time and work under pressure. Sit beside them, encourage them, buy the glue and supplies, but let them do the work. Success will mean little to them if the grade and accolades really belong to their parents.

Social and emotional support during this time is vital. If you have done as I mentioned in the elementary years and taught your children how to observe people and be empathetic, it will help navigate middle school. But then there is a whole new level of social interaction as we get into dating years. Crushes in 5th grade are very different than being asked to the 7th grade dance. Looking for qualities in a significant other should be no different than what you taught them to look for in friends during elementary years. See how things are building? They are just like little blocks. You have to form a firm foundation for them to continue to grow. And they are likely to listen to you if previous advice was helpful. As finding someone who is kind and respectful to others is important in a friend, that is what you are looking for in a significant other. Yes, attraction comes into play as they notice the opposite sex, but your job is to help them navigate a relationship with a new gender, not to push them into intimacy.

Physical intimacy is only one aspect of a marital relationship, and one that gets too much focus. Help your tweens learn to navigate dialogue with someone who piques their interest. Do you remember the kindergarten questions? Do you have any pets, do you have siblings? Those can still work here. But build deeper, more mature options for their repertoire with questions such as "What is your favorite book series?" or "Do you play any sports?" etc. Teach them how to ask about other people's interests while also being able to formulate answers to those questions about themselves. Not only are you building their ability to communicate with others, but you are helping them gain an understanding of themselves. And this is a mighty feat in the middle school years. Yay you! Go parents!!!

There is much you can build upon in the kitchen and I found, in recent discussions with my adult children, why some of the things we did were successful, and others were not. First came a new topic for me, as my tween exclaimed, "I don't like what they are serving for school lunch and I want to pack my lunch." Personally, I never did this as a kid. We always ate at school, and in high school, could walk off-campus to eat. By the time this question was proposed to me, they were old enough to know how to make a simple meal, and I asked myself, *"Do I need to do this for them, or can they do it themselves?"* You've learned enough about me by reading this far to know what my answer was.

"If you want to take food from home that is fine, but you will need to pack it yourself." This did prompt a reminder of having items from all the food groups, and I even hung a food pyramid on the refrigerator. It also challenged me to speak with them more about the grocery list and what items they needed. Now, let me just say that fruit roll-ups as a "fruit" and fish crackers as a "grain" are debates for which you will have to prepare an argument. And why the general idea is that Lunchables® could be considered a nutritious meal is beyond me. I have a vivid memory of standing with my son, looking at the back of the container. We discussed sodium levels, looked at the daily percentage of nutrients, and the list of ingredients. I asked him, "Do you think this will give you energy and what you need to get through your day and practice afterward? What about the price of it compared to other things we can purchase?"

Thankfully, I knew that just saying, "no" would not be enough, as well as knowing that saying, "yes" was not the right (albeit easy) choice. Give them knowledge and the opportunity to use that knowledge so they can be able to make the best decisions. FYI: Little surprises like an occasional purchase of gushers, sneaking a miniature candy into their bag, or writing an encouraging note will improve your cool parenting image immensely!

Cooking together: ugh, this is not something I did well. My intentions were always there, but I've been told that my follow-through was a bit invasive and did not produce the fruit for which I had hoped. Please heed my advice and do as I say, not as I did. Because of my lack of enthusiasm for being in the kitchen, but wishing to eat at home, I came up with a brilliant idea starting in middle school. Each of the kids should take one night per week to plan a meal. There were several successful meals prepared by my kids, but Rachel told me that usually I would try to explain to them what to do and then end up doing it myself so that they were not the ones actually preparing and planning, but just following my directions. This is not building them up for the future. In my desire to be efficient and help them learn the timing of having food ready and hot all together I got in the way. It should have been learned by trial and error, not dictation.

Parents, heed my advice and when you have something you tend to hover over, just walk away. Whether that be cleaning, cooking, laundry, lawn mowing, etc. Allow yourself to walk away and be in another location so they can try and err on their own. Help your children build their skills in the kitchen by encouraging them to learn how to plan and prep. Let them experiment with baking and flavors. These are skills they will use the rest of their life. Help them grow wings, one feather at a time, so they can soar on their own!

I spoke of Gary Smalley's book, *The Five Love Languages of Children,* in chapter two and I highly recommend you read it. To my son, whose primary language is physical touch, a hug, rub on the shoulder or pat on the head was important. And it helped me to know that when he hugged me, he was saying, "I love you." When Noel complimented my food or outfit she was saying, "I love you." As her love language is words of affirmation. And when Rachel invited me on a walk or to sit on the porch, she was saying, "I love you" because her language is quality time. Not only did this book teach me how to express love in a way my children needed to receive it, but it also taught me how to interpret their strengths in loving me. Teen years can be rather barren in the land between parent and child, so I urge you to read Gary's book. It helped me find an oasis in the desert.

Chapter 6: High School
Be Honest

"Free of deceit and untruthfulness; sincere"
Oxford Languages Dictionary

So let me just say that as a parent, I want my children to be honest with me. Therefore, it makes sense that I should be honest with them. Why would I ruin all the years of bonding and building by choosing to be deceitful or lie to them now? Because we are scared that if we tell our children about some of the things we did as a teenager they will make the same mistakes? I understand your fear, but my husband and I found the opposite to be true. We chose not to spill every detail of everything up front, but when they asked questions, we were honest.

And parents, it is very important that you know this: **Your children can learn from your mistakes**. Sharing the errors of your past and why you regret your actions will work to prevent them from repeating them, not drive them to mimic you. Not speaking about them, or hiding hard times only brings mystery, frustration and deceit. Teens do not respond well to dishonesty, especially from their parents. Furthermore, it makes their life seem less lonely to know that Mom and Dad faced many of the same challenges, difficult decisions, and temptations they are navigating.

Bonding

It was a known expectation in our household that when our teens returned from any time away from home, they stopped in to give a brief report to Mom and Dad. Whenever we heard the garage door, we would pause the TV and wait for them to enter. These were fun and typically revealing moments. You could sense a mood from a date, how interactive a party was, or when they felt inspired by a youth group presentation or activity.

It takes me back to my recent chapter about being present. They knew we were always going to be there ready to hear how their event went. I know they often looked forward to sharing information. And then sometimes they hoped we would be asleep or forget to pause the movie so they could sneak past without a report. And sometimes they would give a simple, "Hey! It went fine. I'm tired and going to bed." I do wonder if the knowledge that we would be asking about their evening had any impact on the choices they made.

With my girls, I could often glean that there was more to tell but they did not want Dad to hear. Dad did not want to hear when it was gushy stuff about a guy. A long look or glance at me was an indication to follow them to their room for more information. I admit that sometimes I followed hoping they would tell me more when in actuality they did not. And that was okay. The point was to make them know we cared. We wanted to know what happened outside of our walls, and they knew what they did mattered to us.

Our open communication did not have boundaries on personal topics. I was candid with my kids about the hormones and desires of teens. When Noel said, "Mom, I know you don't like it when I wear my tights without a long shirt, but why? Do they not look good?"

"Yes, they look fantastic on you. You have a nice tush. And a guy will look at you in those tight pants and think, 'That looks good, I'd sure like to get a hold of it.'"

"Mom! I can't believe you said that!"

"Well, go ask your brother and I bet he will agree with me that this is how some guys think."

Her brother confirmed my comment, and I did not have to argue with her about covering her back side again.

Consequently, we had conversations with our son about respecting a woman, and realizing that until he is married, she is someone else's future wife. Same for our girls: this is someone else's husband and you all need to set some boundaries.

Early in their dating relationships I began to ask, "Have you discussed boundaries?" I proceeded to tell them they needed to decide where they plan to draw the line in regard to physical touch and they needed to make that clear to whomever they were dating. I asked that question often and most of the time they left on a date I would say, "Mind your boundaries."

When they inquired about where my limits had been and whether I had issues with these temptations, I was honest. I shared stories about what worked and what did not work in my own life. We had a rule that they were not allowed to be in the house alone with a boyfriend or girl-friend. It worked well for us and we never got a negative response from any of the people they dated. Obviously, this would not prevent our teens from having the thrill of passion overtake them, but it made them think about it. This way it was not ignored until the heat of the moment but addressed early on. They knew it was a choice and they had prepared for what decision they hoped to make. Not bringing up a topic does not prevent your teen from experiencing it. It simply makes them unprepared to re-act to it.

Honest discussions about everything should be an enjoyable part of having teenagers, from politics, to drugs, to homosexuality, to screen use—you name it but have an open discussion. Openness means you have to be willing to hear their side of the story as well as voice your own. If things get heated because you do not agree, I highly recommend you pull out the speaking spoon and make sure you are able to recap what each person says before the next person speaks. As the saying goes, God gave you two ears and one mouth; therefore, you should listen twice as much as you speak.

Another enjoyable way to bond with your high school-ers is to share movies and books that meant something to you at their age. You can do this their whole life, but there is something about getting to those more mature movies which spark conversations and a deeper under-standing of one another. I feel it is always hard for kids to picture their parents as young people. Sharing a movie that touched you in some way, and explaining to them how it impacted you opens their eyes to see you as more than just Mom and Dad. *Breakfast Club* is a great rite of passage movie. There is so much to discern from the stereotypes they bring out, which unfortunately, are still very much alive today. This is why it's so great. The kids can still relate. You can delve into which characters they connect with and why. You can share who you were the most like. It is especially fun to tell the kids you want to share a movie you grew up with and watch their reluctant apprehension. They think it will be boring or uninteresting. When you see them laughing, crying, and enjoying the time it is a delight!

Both the love of books and her love language of quality time were expressed by Rachel in her final year at home. Her father had never read the Harry Potter series and he proclaimed, "I'll listen to it if someone reads it to me." Challenge accepted. At first, Rachel and I took turns reading but her character voices and expressions were far more entertaining than mine. Thus it was that every time the three of us were home together she would read. Jay and I still cherish the profound quality of time and special bond that ensued by the hours we spent listening to our senior in high school read the entire series aloud to us. Allow yourself to be a part of their world and be open to study and learn from your teens. Like a glue that has to permeate the surface to make it stick, you'll create a lasting bond.

Building

The high school years go too fast. Well, life in general goes too fast. But we really had fun during this phase. We were very fortunate that all of our kids liked the same activities. They all did track and cross country. Rachel and Noel both were in some plays and musicals, and all three did show choir one year. It was easier to get involved in the sport when we had two or three kids participating. Because of their age, all three were in high school together for one year (freshman, sophomore, senior). A lot of fun friends came and went. Our car was always packed with blankets and snacks for cold meets and long rides. And our door was always open for long conversations and deep questions.

Do you see how this has built on every phase? Teaching them to share toys, to ask questions, to make friends, and to be involved in their school activities and supporting their activities all culminates into the kids building relationships, families knowing who you are and trusting you enough to send their kids to your home. You have built the foundation for them to keep growing. And it will not stop when they leave the house. They will use these skills to get along with future roommates and spouses. They will be able to negotiate with co-workers and respect their boss. Every chapter of their life builds on the next as they develop their own story, a classic novel for which you are helping them to write.

The relationship building blocks were key for social interaction. Just as the alphabet and opportunities to read and learn are keys to academic success. My kids all made better grades than I did. I consider myself one who has more common sense than book smarts. Many of their classes in high school were beyond my academic ability to help. Our role is about helping them build healthy habits for success as well. Ensuring they eat nutritious food, have good lighting and quiet space when they are studying, and get work done before play were our goals. You need to be prepared to pull your teen from an event or activity if they are not keeping up with their responsibilities. This is something you should discuss prior to them joining new clubs or sports. Do they have time in their schedule to do it?

There was no negotiating the fact that when they turned sixteen, they needed to get a job. Noel was not having this. She turned sixteen in the fall of her sophomore year, and we began to discuss options for her to get a job by summer. She crossed her arms, huffed out annoyances at every option we named and jutted her lower jaw so far out I'm surprised it was not out of joint. She very begrudgingly picked three locations for which she had to apply. I clearly remember driving her to the ice cream shop to pick up an application (online options were not popular yet) and she slammed the door to the car so hard I rocked back and forth. Nonetheless, this was the place where she got hired.

When she went for an interview, her dad and I prepared her with all sorts of questions and she said all they did was ask about her schedule, have her do some math problems and inquire if she knew how to wash dishes. The dishes were the biggest topic as the owner actually had her describe the steps involved in washing dishes. She later shared with Noel, "You'd be surprised at how many kids I interview who have never washed a dish in their life." Don't be that parent! Teach your kids to wash dishes.

Anyway, she had online training for about a month which included passing the health department certification and getting familiar with all the treats made at the shop. And this was paid time. Her first check arrived and suddenly the idea of having a job was not so bad. The shop worked with her schedule for track in the spring and of course her hours were greatly increased during the summer. She ended up working there for almost three years! To this day, she often thanks us for making her get a job and reflects on how much she learned. It was easy to get her siblings in the work force as they saw the financial benefit that ensued.

Financial responsibility is another building block that started with teaching the kids how to manage their $1.00 per week allowance. We kept to the same mantra that they needed to tithe 10%, but we added the rule to make them save 50%. College is expensive and we knew they would need extra funding. But we also know it is hard to work diligently at something and not be able to enjoy the reward. They could use the remaining 40% at their discretion. But this does not mean we ignored any level of advice about wise spending. Some of them chose to save more than 50%. Some spent every penny of the 40%. Although they were making their own money, we continued to purchase any items they **needed**, whereas they had to purchase items they **wanted**.

An example of this was when Noel asked if we would buy her a pair of boots. I responded, "I thought you already had some boots. Did your foot grow, is there a hole in them?"

"No, I just like this newer style better," she replied.

That, my friends, is a want and not a need. So she had to decide if she wanted the new boots bad enough to spend her own money. At the time this just seemed like a practical way to parent. We did not realize how great this impact would be on their future spending. All of our kids, having to use their own money in a decisive way, became very cautious about what they buy. To this day, they ask themselves, "Do I need that, or do I want that?" They shop discount racks, wait to purchase things off-season, and know the value of every penny they earn. Financial building blocks are essential to achieve independence as an adult. Start young and continue the conversations and understanding to build the millionaires of tomorrow.

Our chore chart was still in effect through the teen years. Our thought, even though their schedules were very full and demanding, was that they were part of the family and needed to share in keeping up with regular household chores. This would be true when they became adults. Why should they not learn now how to balance out those responsibilities? But we did give them options. In the real world, if you have work to do and become unable to complete your tasks you have a few options:

- Ask a co-worker to help you.

- Hire an external source to do the work.

- Admit to your boss you are unable to handle the task.

All of these scenarios played out in regard to the small household chores. The kids learned to trade with one another on days when they were busy. Sometimes they paid each other, which was especially lucrative for Rachel (our youngest) once the other two started working. They had extra money and she had extra time. And finally, there were moments when they had a big test, worked extra hours, or simply felt a bit overwhelmed when they would come to us and admit they needed help with their chores that week. Life skills were learned from the simple chores they were assigned as a preschooler and the parental persistence to teach them responsibility and respect.

One final bit of advice on building with communication is the family calendar. You all are so fortunate that you have online options and apps to help with this. I had to hunt each year for the calendar with squares big enough to include all of our activities. But as the online options became available, we did have Google calendars and we shared those with one another so we were all aware of what was going on and how to keep up. I have a friend with seven children and each one has a different color. What I liked about this was that the older kids were able to see when their younger sibling had a track meet or play so they could make plans to attend.

Attendance was something we required of all of them through the years. They had to attend at least one game, concert, or play each season when their sibling was involved in something. Quinn used to complain about going to see his sisters in The Nutcracker every December. But I reminded him that they had sat through more than one baseball game each season. At least the girls only had one performance.

Nonetheless, finding a way to keep track of activities and making the kids be responsible to inform the family of these activities as they get older can really help them prepare for communicating with their future family and friends. My favorite example of this was sharing a grocery list with everyone. When it was just a piece of paper on the fridge, I would often have to call home and ask someone to tell me what was on it because I forgot to take it to the store. But smart phones allowed anyone to have the list at any time. The kids could also only blame themselves if their favorite snack was depleted and they did not add it to the list. Using a shared grocery list with an app like "Cozi" seems so simple, but it encouraged them to be responsible for the outcome they wanted (getting more food) and freed up the parents from having to feel guilty when the milk was gone. The whole family worked together to keep our household on track.

I am going to end with a unique task we did for New Year's. It is both a bonding and a building item and a reminder to all of you that your family is unique. As I shared from the very beginning, this book is not an end-all-be-all parenting know-how. This is a compilation of shared stories and parental experiences that worked for us. It is meant to spark some ideas, encourage persistence through the challenges, and help you to see the long-term outcome of daily patience in being intentional, consistent, instructive, involved, present, and honest parents.

Our special New Year's idea came to me as people were emphasizing resolutions. I've never really been a big fan of New Year's resolutions. They so often seem like empty promises we make, or lofty goals which have little chance to succeed. I became determined to come up with an alternative idea for our new year. About that same time I was in a group and became involved with creating a new mission statement for them. This brought an aha moment and I discussed it with my husband. We decided that instead of creating an individual resolution for the year, to create a family motto. With our kids we talked about what a motto or mission statement was, read the samples from both of our places of employment and spent some time discussing our family. It was great! We talked about what we do, how we want to help others, contemplated how others see us, questioned if there was anything we needed to push ourselves toward, and created a motto. We hung it on the fridge and tried to remind ourselves to live up to it in the coming year. We revisited it again and tweaked it the following year and the year after that. But then, we decided it did not need to be changed. We liked this one and it has been our motto for at least nine years. It is hanging on our refrigerator right now. I think it sums up all we worked for as parents and is a great way to end my chapter.

> The Endicott Family Motto: "The Endicott family will seek to do our best, treat people as we would like to be treated, ask forgiveness when wrong and love others with Christ like love."

When it comes down to it, we can all create ideal conditions for our children. We can strengthen bonds, build them up in every way possible and create a motto, but it is up to each individual to make the right choices. Parents, all we can do is our best. There are no guarantees. My grandmother in-law, Marie Endicott, painted a small bird on a tree branch with an anonymous quote that reads, "There are two lasting bequests we can give our children; one is roots, the other is wings." May yours choose to fly in a good direction when they leave the nest. And may you rest assured knowing you did everything possible to grow their feathers and raise kind, independent, productive citizens.

Chapter 7: Belief

*"Faith is being sure of what we hope
for and certain of what we do not see."*
Hebrews 11:1 (NIV)

If you have read up to this point you are likely aware
that I am a Christian. I mention church and praying
over things throughout the book, but in this chapter, I
am going to dig deeper into the pivotal role my faith
played in each phase of parenting. I grew up in a Christian home and have believed in God my entire life. I
had a near death experience at the age of six that sealed
my belief in God and started my daily interactions of
prayer and discernment which continue to guide me
now.

Having three children in less than three years is not
a path most of us choose, but it is the one which was
laid before me. Our nearest relative was over two hours
away. My church friends were my family and provided
the support I needed to endure challenging times and
activities together to laugh and grow through life.

In all honesty, I do not know how people get through
hard times in life without faith. My father died of can-
cer when I was pregnant with my first child. I was close
to my dad and depended on him a lot for advice and

help. Growing up, I was much more comfortable in the garage than the kitchen. His loss was great, but I knew he was with my Heavenly Father, and I still feel his presence when I need encouragement.

If you have experienced loss or heartache in your life, I encourage you to open to the book of Psalms, which is right in the middle of the Bible, and read any chapters that are revealed to you. People cry out with frustration and anguish in the Psalms. People rejoice and sing praises of joy throughout the Psalms. When I do not know what to do or how to feel, I read from Psalms and am always amazed how the words speak to me and can express what I am feeling or renew my soul in a most inspiring way.

My hope for all of you is that these explanations of how we incorporated our faith into the lives of our children, how we sought guidance from God in all we did for our kids, and how we dedicated their lives to His service will inspire you. Belief and acting out our faith is the true reason we found success as parents. May it be a calming and guiding presence for you.

Couple First

I did not mention this at the beginning of the book. It is, after all, a book about being a parent. But I would be remiss to not express the importance of being a couple first. You, Mom and Dad, are the core foundation of your family. If you do not take time to build your own relationship together and together with Christ, the foundation is susceptible to cracks. Know your spouse, honor your spouse, do things for your spouse even when you don't feel like it. Keep communication open and learn how to agree with and support one another so that you can approach your children on a united front. My husband and I pray together on a regular basis every morning and every night. Sometimes we simply recite the Lord's prayer together. Typically one of us prays for a few minutes. Occasionally, we banter on whose turn it is to pray. But it is rare for us to miss a morning or evening. It is an important part of our relationship which has kept us together for over thirty years. And those prayers always include each of our children.

Infant

Oh the precious moments of holding a newborn in your arms and the special connection of their silent, peaceful slumber. As they lay helpless in your arms, pray over them. I used to do a head-to-toe prayer. It would sound something like this:

> Lord, bless this child. You know every hair on their head. Protect them from the evils of the world. Help their mind to grow in knowledge and wisdom about you and compassion for others. Create a desire to learn and bless them with good teachers throughout their lives.
>
> Bless their eyes that they may see others as you do and that reading is a gift and offers insight. Help them to see reality while being protected from violent, harmful images.
>
> Bless their nose that they never turn it up toward others or look down upon those with a different upbringing from their own.

Bless their ears to hear and to listen. Oh, Lord, help them listen more than they speak and especially to hear your voice and know when to follow words of wisdom and not an ill-intended crowd. Help them to hear the small, important, and kind voices over the loud rumblings of deceit and lies.

Bless their mouth to speak words of kindness and peace. Grant them wisdom and control over their tongue that it will not lash others with harsh words. If it be your will, give them the gift of wisdom and the ability to share it with others. Help them to be confident when placed in front of a crowd and guide the words they share in all circumstances.

Bless their body Lord. Help it to be strong and able to work to help others. Give them a kind and generous heart whose passion matches your own. Keep it healthy and sensitive to the world around them.

I pray you send them love, Lord; friends and a spouse to love with deep passion and compassion. Protect their womb and ability to procreate Lord.

Send barriers to block promiscuity and help them to honor you in all their actions.

Keep their arms and legs strong and guide them in the path toward you. Send people into their lives to guide them as they walk through their journey. May their hands produce good work for you and the kingdom. May their legs be strong enough to carry others who need help along the journey of life.

Lord, I pray that it is your will for them to have a strong and healthy body that will grow to love and honor you.

Give me the strength and wisdom to guide them in this life. Thank you for blessing me with this beautiful child. Help me honor you with them every day. Amen.

That was the head-to-toe prayer I uttered often with my children. I still sometimes pray this when I am thinking of them and do not have a specific prayer or need in mind. And I will admit that more than once, I have fallen asleep without getting through their entire body.

Being able to acknowledge what we want for our children with the Lord is very important. Being able to offer our child to the Lord to guide them and trusting His will in all aspects of their lives is equally important. Pray for yourself and daily sustenance as parenting is labor intense, and I am not just speaking about the birthing process. Remember to take time for quiet moments and scripture readings as this is how the Lord speaks to us. I did not do this enough and sometimes found myself drained in trying to carry the load alone. Give it to the Lord. He is waiting to carry all your burdens.

"Humble yourselves, therefore, under God's mighty hand, that he may lift you up in due time. Cast all your anxiety on him because he cares for you." James 5: 6-7 (NIV).

And don't be too hard on yourself if you fall asleep while praying. God understands our exhaustion.

Preschool

When they were little, we had a chunky children's Bible with vibrant colors and a lot of pictures. These had all the basic Bible stories typically summed up in a page or two of large font. This is how we introduced our children to the Bible. We read with them and prayed with them each night. We built the foundation. As their language developed through the toddler years, they began to ask questions. I remember Rachel giggling one night as I prayed, "Dear Lord, please bless the young boy who will be her husband one day. May he grow up in a kind, loving home and know who you are…." I inquired why she was giggling.

She said, "Who are you praying for?"

I said, "I don't know their name, but I am praying for whomever you may marry one day."

She replied, "How can you pray for them if you do not know them?"

I assured her, "God knows them, and He can prepare them to meet you one day."

This was followed up by a conversation about things she might like in a partner someday. The Lord answered those prayers, because she found a wonderful mate in her husband, Parker, and he does have some of the qualities she mentioned as a young girl. His mother shared that she too was praying from the time Parker was young that he would find the partner God intended for his life. Prayers are not always answered quickly, and it is okay to pray for things that are years in the future. God hears them all and takes joy in listening.

> "This is the confidence we have in approach-
> ing God: that if we ask anything according
> to his will, he hears us." 1 John 5:14 (NIV).

Our family attended church every Sunday. We ini-
tially went to a congregation about thirty minutes from
our home in a neighboring county. This is where my
husband and I had attended before our children were
born and when we lived just a couple miles away. We
loved our church family there and were very connected with some of the families, but the distance made it
more challenging to be involved, especially with kids'
naps and bedtime schedules. We also watched the youth
group planning a Spring Break trip and realized that
our kids would not be in the same school district. Their
break would be different than the kids at church, and
the kids at school would not be kids from their church.
This, along with discerning prayer, led us to seek out a
new church as a family.

I found it to be a very strengthening time for us.
Although they were young, our children knew what
made them comfortable and feel excited about being
at church. We quickly narrowed it down to two con-
gregations. We alternated going to one each Sunday
and talking about how it went. The kids shared about
Sunday School: the teachers they heard and children
they met. My husband and I discussed what we thought
of the groups we interacted with, and we pondered the
worship music, sermon and style. In the end, we had a
unanimous agreement to attend Wilmore United Meth-
odist Church. It was a great place for our family. The
children's ministry leaders had a big influence on their
young lives while the youth pastor and head pastor
provided strong, positive influences in their formative

years. They attended many retreats and mission trips together.

My husband and I have gained much wisdom through our Sunday School classes and I meet about once a month with some women in my congregation who help me get through all of life's challenges. I'm sure we would have grown in either congregation, but talking through this change as a family helped solidify our bond and was an easy way to work together on a task which produced great fruit for all of us. Discuss life events with your children. Listen to their wisdom regarding such things. You may be surprised at how insightful your children can be.

Elementary

At some point during the cold, winter days of elementary years we decided to try to read the Bible together. Not just verses here and there, but the whole Bible!! I think our church had handed out guides to follow which would give specific chapters each night to read in order to make it through in a year. It was quite entertaining. We took turns reading out loud and some of the Old Testament stories about incest and other promiscuous behavior brought comments of "That is disgusting" and "Why are we reading this?" As well as comparisons in the New Testament with forgiveness of both self and others and how many problems of biblical times are much like current issues we face. Often the conversations after the reading brought more insight than the scripture itself.

I admit that we did not make it far. Some nights, because of the conversation, we did not make it through the readings. We eventually became so far behind it did not seem practical to catch up. Then we had distractions with other activities and spring schedules which left us little time to all five be together and in the proper mood to sit and listen to one another read. It was well-intended and brought some insight and growth to our family. I encourage you to try it with yours. You may find more success.

I share this with you to help you see that my parenting was not perfect. I often fell short of goals or lacked the discipline to follow through, but that does not mean I failed. Effort is a great reason why we eventually find success. If you do not give an effort toward something, you are guaranteed to fail. And even the few weeks we did read together brought time of bonding and building. Look at what you gain in trying. Don't focus on forcing something just to say you did it. Be willing to accept that sometimes you need to shift gears or the family shifts them for you. Look at what went well and dive into the next opportunity to create a connection and growth.

Our church had a special fifth grade recognition where parents were encouraged to write a letter to their children about their faith journey. It was kind of an opportunity to sum up their life thus far and share our hopes for the future. Those letters are still very important to our children, serving as reminders of our love and commitment to them. Those framed letters hung on their walls for years. I think they were like a baton in a relay race. We are still part of the same team, but we are handing off the baton for them to take control of their own faith. They need to own the path they will forge in moving forward. I never really thought of the significance of that until just now, but it truly is how things transition as they begin to be part of a youth group and build deeper relationships with people outside of your family. Keep showing them how to be faithful by modeling your own faith. Let them see you read scripture. Share with them how they can pray for you. When I asked my kids to pray for me during those years it was beautiful to hear them speak to the Heavenly Father on my behalf.

Middle School

Middle School is a pivotal time. It is natural in this pre-teen time to create bigger bonds with friends and begin pulling away from time with family. Friendship in middle school will greatly influence the ease of these years. Prayers for wisdom in the relationships they choose cannot be fervent enough.

Noel always had a good group of friends and seemed to make friends easily. From church youth group to school extracurricular activities to the neighborhood, her connections made her happy and in general she made wise choices in her friends. We had many fun sleepovers and various co-ed gatherings during those years with all three kids.

Rachel had a core group of gal pals who dubbed themselves "the blonde squad" even though only two of them were actually blonde. This group of girls had one another's back. They alternated homes for slumber parties, giggled incessantly and shared very deeply with one another. Her middle school years were easier because she had people who understood and supported her.

Quinn had a more challenging time in middle school. I think it was a combination of tremendous pressure he put on himself with performing in track and cross-country and feeling he had to lead his team, and a relationship he was developing with a young lady who had a different group of friends. He got caught up trying to prove himself in two worlds rather than finding a group of close friends who could help him accept the person he was. Those were some trying times, and much of what he experienced was not realized by us until later. But he has confessed that he always knew his dad and I were there for him. He always felt love and guidance from us. He said he was blown away by our reaction when he shared some deep issues because he expected us to be angry or disappointed. He reflected, "Your loving response helped me understand how God loves us unconditionally and that strengthened my bond with you."

Some parenting moments we can't predict or prepare for. But the emphasis throughout this book on bonding and building will create the core foundation to help you all survive any storms that blow your way. By the grace of God, we weathered all those child-rearing days without losing our foundation.

The biggest foundation goes back to the very beginning of this chapter where I described my prayer for the helpless infant in my arms. Helpless is often how we felt through the teenage years. The kids often do not want to talk, grow angry when you ask questions, or hide things from you so it is impossible to know how to help or what to say. Patience and prayer are your guide. And to those who do not yet have teenagers, I want you to know that yes, they are hard years. But they are also wonderful years. We had many, many incredible, deep, fun memories with our teenage children. It is a gift to see them becoming independent adults. But getting to those good moments takes patience and prayer. I can't emphasize this enough. If you are not patient, it will ruin many opportunities to connect to your kids. If you are not praying over them and for yourself, it would be like steering a train without any tracks.

My husband started a new job the year we had two children in middle school and one in 5th grade. This new position had him traveling about 50% of the time. This was a big adjustment! Six months after this major shift, I was offered a full-time position. I had not worked full-time since before my children were born. I shared the job description with my kids and my son said, "Mom, this totally sounds like you. I think you should do it." We discussed what it would mean to our family.

"You kids would have to do more around the house," I told them. They acknowledged that they would be willing to help more with chores. Of course the fact that the extra income would also mean a new pair of track shoes or ability to eat out more often may have had some influence on accepting extra chores. Fortunately, the hours of this position were somewhat flexible. It involved occasional evenings and weekends, which meant I could leave early to pick the kids up from school, or drive to out-of-town track meets and choir concerts. Adjusting to all of this life change was a whirlwind of challenges. Just as my kids were exploring bigger and broader changes, my husband was not there to talk to, and I did not have as much time to contemplate what was happening or keep up with household chores.

"Lord, what do I do?"

PRAY!

Many nights I sat in the hallway outside of their rooms, sometimes when they were still awake and busy studying. I would pray over everything I wanted to say, all that was weighing on my heart, and all the ways I felt inadequate. I learned something very important during those teenage years of prayer, PATIENCE. If something came up that I felt I needed to talk to my kids about, I learned to pray first and patiently wait upon the Lord.

"I really feel I need to talk to them about _____. I think it is bothering them and I feel I can offer some insight in this way," I would tell the Lord.

The Lord would softly reply in my heart, "Be patient."

I would pray about this issue. It would weigh on me, and I would keep picturing my encounter with my child on how I would address the issue. But the Lord would say, "Be patient."

If I was able to contain myself, inevitably the kids would bring up the topic somehow and I knew that was my moment to share all that I had been preparing to say. Most of the time it was well received and would allow us to have a deeper conversation on the issue. In the reverse, if I was not patient, felt my knowledge was best because I was the parent, and rushed to share my fabulous insight when they were not ready to hear it, it did not go well. The kids would typically become angry or resentful, sometimes even hurt that I brought this subject to their attention. All my preparation went down the tube because I did not wait for the right moment.

It is hard to choose a specific story on this because they were all so personal and diverse. Some were simple things like hygiene habits, but others were very deep subjects, like birth control and physical boundaries. Whenever I felt led to say something on a subject I knew might be a bit controversial, or argumentative, I asked the Lord for an opening. He never failed me. Sometimes it would be immediate…like within an hour. I'd be praying about talking to them and they would walk in and ask a question on the subject or tell me a story about a friend who had an issue similar to what I was wanting to share. Other times it might be weeks or months before the timing was right. Don't misinterpret this as a time to ignore a major issue with your child. Some things have to be addressed even if it makes us all uncomfortable. But if it is a subject that is more of a life lesson or a *Mom and Dad think you need to know this* topic, it can likely wait. Give it a lot of prayer and ask for long-term patience so you can share when they are willing to hear. I promise the results will be worth it!

High School

Prayers for dating relationships were vital during this time. It was rare for all three of our kids to be single at the same time. Being so close in age was actually an advantage to us because they typically knew the people their siblings were dating and did not hesitate to share their opinions of such relationships. We found it extremely important to have the significant others over to our house. If the purpose of dating is to eventually find someone with whom you are compatible so that you can spend the rest of your life together, then it is equally important to ensure they are compatible with your family. After all, family will be a part of your life for all of your life.

It was revealing to us and to them how these individuals interacted with the family. Sometimes we really liked the people they dated and it was hard when they broke up. Some brought great relief when our child recognized the challenges we all saw from the beginning. In each of these circumstances, there is heartache and perhaps some confusion. I always told my kids, "Think of all the things you liked about this person and know that God has someone even better for you in the future." It was encouraging to see them learn about themselves and the qualities they wanted in a partner. We also expressed the importance of being content in singleness. Marriage is not for everyone, and it is vital for people to learn to be content with themselves. If you do not enjoy your own company, it can be challenging for others to enjoy being around you as well. Strengthening your own, individual relationship with God is key during these high school years and we found a strong youth group to be very helpful in this endeavor.

One of our kids found a stronger connection and growth opportunity at a different church youth group. This is okay. We would much prefer them to find a place where they can grow than to feel they had to stay at our church and not find a spiritual mentor or peers who challenged them to grow closer to Christ. As your teenager turns into an adult, support their questions about who God is and how they fit into the world as a whole.

Pray over their choices, but do not force them to follow the exact path you did. None of our children chose to attend the church they grew up in, but all of them choose to go to church. This is a tremendous blessing and we are so grateful they, along with their spouses, plan to raise their own kids with a weekly routine of praising God within a congregation who can walk with them in their spiritual journey. "Train your child in the way" but be willing to let them choose their own path.

Speaking of spiritual journey, along with high school comes the decision of college or career. We actually told our kids from a young age that once they turned eighteen, they would have three choices:

- Go to college

- Join the military

- Start paying rent

When my daughter shared this with a high school co-worker the girl responded, "That is mean. Your parents are really strict. I can't believe they would just kick you out."

Noel replied, "They would not kick me out, but they would make me get a job and start paying rent. They just don't want me to be lazy and stay home doing nothing."

Of course *I* don't think this was a mean ultimatum. I was part of the parent team who enforced this policy and I think it worked. None of our kids had to pay us rent. They all chose to go to college, and they all graduated within four years. They knew what the expectation was from a very young age. And they knew we would follow-through with our expectations. Decide early on what you and your spouse will accept from your children when they graduate from high school. Be clear in communicating this to your kids and be prepared to follow through with the plan.

All of our kids were able to go to a Christian Liberal Arts University. We were tremendously blessed to work in conjunction with Asbury University and Asbury Seminary so that their tuition was free. Yes, folks, this was an incredible gift and believe me, we and our kids know how tremendous this gift was. Two of the kids graduated from Asbury, but Rachel felt she needed to create her own environment and transferred to a much larger, state school. When she approached us she said, "I actually feel I would be disobeying God if I stayed where I am."

That is a hard argument for which we could not disagree. We discussed the fact that without the free tuition she would have to incur some of the debt herself. She knew what she was getting into. And she has expressed multiple times how much she appreciated our support of this decision rather than forcing her to stay where we thought was more sensible financially. This transfer even helped strengthen her faith because she prayed for and found a strong Christian group on campus that provided some wonderful friendships and faith building experiences in her life, experiences that were a better option for her.

Money management is just as much a part of spiritual guidance as everything else. The Lord calls us to be good stewards. This is not just with finances. We should be good stewards of our time, our gifts, our belongings.

All we have is from the Lord and we need to honor Him with it. Teach your children to honor God by giving him the first fruits of their labor. This is the 10% we always made them tithe. I have a great deal of respect for my husband in this matter. Even when our finances were at our tightest (and we had some very lean years), he never even considered that we would stop tithing. We have always had what we needed; food, clothing and shelter. We let our kids know that other things in life are a bonus and while I feel the Lord blesses us and wants us to enjoy our time on Earth, He expects us to be generous and wise in how we spend our gifts.

If you have the opportunity, teach your children about investing and saving. Let them grasp compound interest and what it can do for them if they start a habit of saving now. Don't be afraid to have honest discussions about what you and your spouse did well and where you had weakness. Again, let them learn from your mistakes. Those honest talks open the door for them to feel they can come to you if they do have struggles. Because they know you will not judge them. They know you had trials in your younger years as well.

There are dozens of examples I could share with you regarding the evidence of faith and God's blessings in our lives. There are also many examples of tension, frustration, arguments, and miscommunication. Joys and sorrows are both a part of life.

It is time for me to come to a close and to allow you to put some of these ideas into practice. I hope you will allow yourself to be human in your parenting and accept that none of us can do it perfectly. Enjoy your children and make the most of each day. Find strength in the Lord to see you through the challenges and give Him praise when the blessings flow.

From Stan Key's book *Face To Face*, there is a study on September 10th titled "Ready, Aim, Fire!" King Solomon, in Psalm 127, compares soldiers' bows and arrows with parents and children. Mr. Key goes on to say:

> <u>He makes them ready</u>. Making the arrow was both science and art. Each one was unique, custom-made for a specific mission.

> <u>He aims.</u> The warrior waited for just the right moment. Timing was crucial. An apt description of much parenting today is contained in the couplet: "I shot an arrow into the air, it fell to earth I know not where." If aim is poor or the target ill-conceived, all the effort of preparation will be wasted.

> <u>He fires.</u> Arrows are not meant to be collected or displayed, nor are they meant to be hoarded in the quiver. They are meant to be fired. Letting go of our children is just as much a God-ordained responsibility as forming them and giving them direction. Once launched, children discover that God has equipped them with an internal guidance system that permits them to make in-flight modifications. Though mom and dad's influence were great, now they must take full responsibility for the trajectory of their life's path.

This is your purpose. You are preparing your arrows, each one uniquely, to be able to fly. I hope you can learn from my efforts in focusing on prayer and patience through the good and challenging times of parenting. Know that you are not alone in the endeavor to raise spirit-filled women and men in an age of individualism and self-focused greed. I have prayed over this book and every individual who will pick it up so that you will be prepared to fire your arrows. From the forming of ideas to every word I typed, to this very day; you are being prayed over and I hope you feel the empowerment to parent well.

In closing this chapter, I will leave you with a final comparison. While sitting through a recent sermon at First Baptist Church in Seymour, Indiana, I heard Pastor Jeremy say, "Do the mundane and ordinary things well." He went on to compare this to athletes and how "…you have to be firm in fundamentals to be successful."

I suppose that is why I want this book to succeed. It has the fundamentals of how we found success as parents and that is what I want for all parents. We must do the daily, mundane things well in order to see the great success of having a confident, kind, productive adult child who lives their life for the Lord and who, only by God's grace, considers us a good parent.

Conclusion
Dad's Perspective

Christine asked me to contribute some thoughts to this book which is truly an honor. As her husband and parental partner I have had a front row seat to the development of our three adult children through their various stages of life. Parenting is one of the hardest jobs, and yet one of the most rewarding. You are given a chance to pour yourself into teaching and shaping another human being. Whether a single parent with the help of relatives or friends, or a couple, it still takes teamwork for successful parenting. Even before we married, Christine and I talked about how we would parent. We discussed how many children we may want, how we should discipline and how it was important to raise them with confidence, compassion and a strong faith that would guide them. This takes open communication, patience, forgiveness and trust, important areas to invest time for yourself and each other.

Being intentional is important for successful parenting but it is also important to be flexible. As I have shared with my children, in the seas of life we set a course, but adjust for the wind with God as our compass. Successful parenting must have a plan, but it must be flexible and adjusted as needed. Christine and I talked often about what worked or didn't work. It helped that she was the planner and came up with some wonderful ideas, many that worked well. However, once in a while, some spontaneity livened things up, providing memorable moments, whether it was a puppet play, romping in the snow, going on a hike, wrestling on the floor or just breaking into singing silly songs or dancing together. Appreciate the spontaneity of your own children and remember they are part of your team too. Once when Christine was stressed with three little ones in diapers and sat with her hands covering her face, little toddler Rachel waddled over, pulled her hands apart and declared, "Peek-a-boo, Mommy!" That spontaneous comment brought some laughter providing much relief and showed that even little Rachel had something to contribute.

"Bonding" is crucial for building any team and that is especially true for a family. Your priorities are spoken clearly by actions and children know where they stand. Does the news, game, movie, or work take precedent over your child or spouse? Earlier in this book Christine shared that if you want a child's respect as a teen you must gain it as a toddler. That is so true. Another phrase I've heard that captures this is "People don't care what you know until they know you care." Once when Quinn was three years old and in part-time daycare, I told him I would take him out early so we could go fishing for his birthday. He shared later as a teen how he was so excited that day for his dad to come and get him so we could spend time fishing together. At that time, I may not have realized how much that action spoke to my small son, but it did and is just one small example of many ways a parent can show their children that they matter.

As a parenting team we are hopefully "building" children into successful adults. As we are intentional in our parenting, we create bonding opportunities to build blocks of knowledge and skills. These bonding moments are built on trust, a trust in the parents and in the family which begins at infancy and continues through life. For us there were many building blocks that were core to our family's foundation such as shared evening meals, chore charts, family meetings, the fifth-grade blessings, a family motto, and participating in a faith community, among others. Sometimes implementing these blocks were met with groans but they made a difference. When Noel went away to college we were thrilled when she would call us with questions because she trusted our wisdom on navigating relationships or dealing with her finances. She was grateful for the skills we taught her as she was now "adulting," as she called it. We had helped build that foundation of trust and skills she began appreciating as she entered adulthood.

So many parents feel the need to make their children happy, at all costs. The long-term goal of the parent should not be to make a child happy. After all, they are only children, and you are their parent who has much more life experience and wisdom. Rather, the role of the parent is to raise confident, kind, and productive members of society. In that process there may be moments of unhappiness, but those are character building moments and believe me, they will appreciate you later in life for them. As Christine shared earlier, my grandmother Endicott declared in her painting; "There are only two bequests we can leave our children; one is roots and the other is wings." May we indeed as parents help provide a solid foundation, the deep roots of our children's lives, so they are confident enough in who they are to soar as they seek their own path in this world. Yet may they be secure enough in our love to know they can always fly home.

Final Words

Okay parents. That is all we have to share (for now). I've given you my best advice and tried to organize it in a way that shows good progression and simple ideas you can adapt. Now it is up to you to implement the information you have gained. Do the hard things; like turning off the screen, talking openly, and saying, "no". Your parenting goals may be different from mine, but you can tweak them which can result in progress for all of you in the game of life.

Remember to bond with your kids by interacting with them, giving them clear boundaries, and getting to know who they are. You have to spend time together to know and understand one another. And you have to learn how to communicate and know what they are saying to you. Discovering their love language is a key factor in being able to bond. Letting go of your own plan for what you want them to be or do is a big start for many parents. Give them opportunities to show you their strengths and talents. Through games, books, and being involved in their activities you will find many ways to build stronger bonds.

Build them up in every phase of life. Think about what they need for their life skills of reading, communicating with people, taking care of a houschold, cooking, managing finances, and general decision making. Let them gradually learn how to grow in all of these areas. While each phase takes intentionality and effort, you learn to build and grow together. Don't underestimate your ability to become creative and think outside the box. Of course, there are many resources that offer ideas for cold, rainy days. You'll get to embrace your own inner child as you play alongside your children.

While I shared a specific word for each phase of parenting, they can all apply to the lifelong journey of becoming a great life coach! Be intentional and consistent so they learn what is expected in your home. Be instructive and involved so they become confident in your support. And be present and honest to build their trust, offering an ongoing haven where they can pour out their heart, sharing their challenges and joys. Parenting is not easy, but it can be fun, rewarding, and a life-giving experience. Remember that your children are a most precious and priceless gift. Cherish them and put the time into raising them well. The return from your investment will be immeasurable.

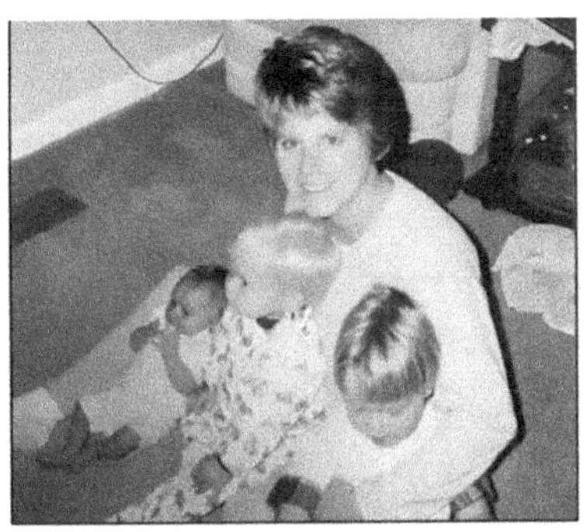

About the Author

Christine is the mother of three adult children; Noel, Quinn, and Rachel, who were all born within 34 months, and mother-in-law to Adonee (Noel), Molly Beth (Quinn) and Parker (Rachel). She has been married to her husband, Jay, for 30 years and is a new grandma to Leon James Marpna. In her free time she enjoys traveling, hiking, writing, board games, and puzzles. Originally from Columbus, Indiana, and a graduate of Ball State University, Christine currently serves as the Director of Conference Services at Asbury University and resides in Wilmore, Kentucky, where she helped coordinate the hospitality for thousands of visitors during the recent Asbury Outpouring\Revival in February of 2023.

If you found this book helpful please email your questions and comments to christine@beaparent.info. You can also visit her website at http://www.beaparent.info for more information

www.ingramcontent.com/pod-product-compliance
Lightning Source LLC
Chambersburg PA
CBHW070613170726
48004CB00018B/1306